CONTENTS

ACKNOWLEDGEMENTS

This book, Golfing in the Zone: The Long Game, is an effort to help all golfers, from professionals to high handicappers, take their game to a higher level of play. There were several people who encouraged this author to put his ideas and techniques into written form. A heartfelt thanks to the following people:

For encouragement and support:
Eric and Melinda Bollinger, Gerry Norquist and J.D. Ebersberger.

For the video and illustrative shotmaking:
Gerry Norquist and Wendy Stuart.

For the camera work, graphics and formatting help :
Daniel Villareal and Bob Brooks.

For helping with the mental tips:
Barry Newman

FOREWORD

By Dave Hill
Former PGA Tour and current Senior Tour Professional

Many golfers dream of becoming better players. The problem is that they don't know if their dreams can become reality. Even if their dreams could become real, they don't understand how to achieve those dreams.

> Dreams are mental fantasies;
> Goals become physical actions.
> Both dreams and goals are necessary.
> But, unless some physical action occurs,
> Dreams will never develop into goals.

LEARN and **TRUST** the fundamentals described and illustrated in this book. Watch your swing improve. Develop the mental processes given for shotmaking. Those of you who do will be amazed at the results achieved by developing and implementing a solid thought process to go along with sound mechanical fundamentals.

LEARN the set-up procedure and the pre-shot routine described in this book. Have a positive belief in the decision you make to play the shot at hand. Have a clear image of the shot, i.e., see the shape of the shot needed to get to the landing area. Set up accordingly. And, then let it happen.

The mental process incorporates: **F-A-C-E:** Focus And Commit to and Execute the shot to be played. Raise your confidence level and reduce your scores by practicing the techniques described in this book. Trust them.

To strike a golf ball well consistently, you need to develop a repeating swing. To develop a repeating swing, you need to understand the basic fundamentals of the mechanics of the swing. You also need to have a perception of the mental processes for solid execution of the shots. Once you learn and understand how to develop these mechanical and mental processes, you will begin to have control of your mind and body. It is this understanding and control that is responsible for lowering your scores and your handicap.

It is important that you spend time mastering the mechanical and thought processes provided In this book. It will make a difference.

wind 8-10 mph

←water

260 yards

230 yds

35 yds

deep rough

light rough

THOUGH-MECHANICAL PROCESS FOR A GIVEN SIT-UATION: Focus on the shape of the highest percentage shot, to get to the landing area.

SHOT SELECTED TO PLAY: Hold-shot against the wind. A draw shot could be adversely affected by wind and end up in the deep rough.

club selection
3-Wood

Par. 4.
410 yards

Pre-F-A-C-E

To many golfers, golf is a religion. And, when one practices religious beliefs, one is normally guided by the teachings and inspirations in the Bible.

According to *Webster's New World Dictionary of the American Language*, the Bible is regarded as an authoritative book that teaches us how to live our lives and also provides a source of guidance and inspiration on how to live a good life. This book, *Golfing in the Zone: The Long Game*, is a teaching tool and a guide on how to play better golf.

The Bible **F**ocuses on teachings through the scriptures and gospel messages. And, it also suggests that by **C**ommitting our lives to understanding right and wrong, and **E**xecuting our lives accordingly, we may have a greater sense of fulfillment and well being.

Since golf is a religion and a way of life to many, *Golfing in the Zone: The Long Game* is designed to illustrate the differences between right and wrong as they pertain to the long game. In *Golfing in the Zone: The Long Game*, we suggest that golfers become accustomed to the acronym **F-A-C-E**, which stands for **F**ocus **A**nd **C**ommit to and **E**xecute the shot to be played and ingrain the concept into their mind. If golfers use this concept in their practice session, they will develop and strengthen their play on the course.

To play good golf, all golfers need to not only lower scores, but also derive a personal fulfillment and pleasure or satisfaction from the game. Golf is a game and should be fun.

This book will provide the golfer with a sense and feel that goes beyond the physical, so the golfer "sees" more clearly how the long game should be played to achieve personal fulfillment. Good golf requires a clarity that goes beyond just the mechanical. *Golfing in the Zone: The Long Game*, conveys this clarity through **F-A-C-E**: **F**ocus **A**nd **C**ommit to and **E**xecute the shot at hand.

When golfers achieve this level of clarity, they are then "golfing in the zone." "Seeing" more clearly activates the visual system more acutely. The visual system provides us with more information than any other means. This is the reason that the principles of **F-A-C-E** are stressed over and over again throughout this book. It is this "seeing" that allows the information received to register in the golfer's brain in an uncluttered manner. "Seeing" mandates that golfers give all of their attention to the focusing and commitment processes.

"Seeing" with greater clarity is a good way to train your mind by "tricking" it. While this sounds a bit strange, look at the following illustration and you will see what I mean. Initially, the image looks like a random pattern of black and white shapes. However, if you follow the instructions, you will find that the mish-mash has some order to it. What is happening is that your visual sense is receiving information and when you close your eyes, the brain processes that information, and in turn, "sees" an image out of the random pattern.

In golf, when a golfer can process information about a shot to be played just a clearly as in the example, then he is "seeing" more acutely what is necessary for the successful completion of the shot. When this happens regularly, the golfer is "in the zone." There is no clutter. There is infinite trust in his ability to not only "see" the shot, but also to execute it. This is what focusing on the moment (or staying in the present) and having a positive belief in yourself really means. It is a way to fine-tune your mental process.

WHAT DO YOU SEE?

Concentrate on the four dots in the middle of the picture for about 30 seconds. Then close your eyes and tilt your head back. Keep them closed. You will see a circle of light. Continue looking at the circle. What do you see?

The concept of **F-A-C-E** is a key element to training the mind—a mind-memory approach. Focus, commitment, concentration, relaxation - these are terms used by most accomplished players after hitting a good shot or playing a solid round. Golfers often explain a good round by saying, "I was in the zone today."

The converse can also be true. The lack of these mental processes can ruin shots. For example, many golfers have experienced a negative thought either just prior to starting the backswing (and not stopping and starting over) or during it. The last second, "don't hit it in the water" thought can enter the golfer's mind. Sometimes, they let these negative thoughts get in the way during the focus and commitment stages. The result is poor execution of the shot.

Disciplining oneself for using the principles of **F-A-C-E** provides a way to better control the mind (and nerves). It can provide a way for golfers to have — a true belief in themselves — a more or less subconscious way of playing the game; a way where only positive thoughts are allowed — no clutter.

On your next round of golf try the following affirmations and thought processes:

- Today, I am happy and calm.

- Today, I shall only let good vibrations (vibes) enter my mind.

- I am going to focus while preparing for every shot, regardless of whether there is a generous fairway from the tee, or a narrow, tree lined one, regardless of whether the pin placement is in the middle of the green, or tucked near the water on the right.

- I shall maintain a consistent pace throughout the round.

- I will deep breath to help relieve tension, improve my focus, and quiet my nerves.

- Between shots, I shall enjoy looking at the clouds and the trees, or observing the fish that swim in the ponds.

- I shall *focus on the moment*.

- I shall stick with my pre-shot routine. If for some reason I am distracted, I shall start my pre-shot process over again.

- I am a winner, therefore I must *think like a champion*.

These affirmations are only some of the things that **F-A-C-E** is all about. Remember that you can implement these practices and concepts on the practice tee as well as on the golf course. Try it, and you will see an improvement.

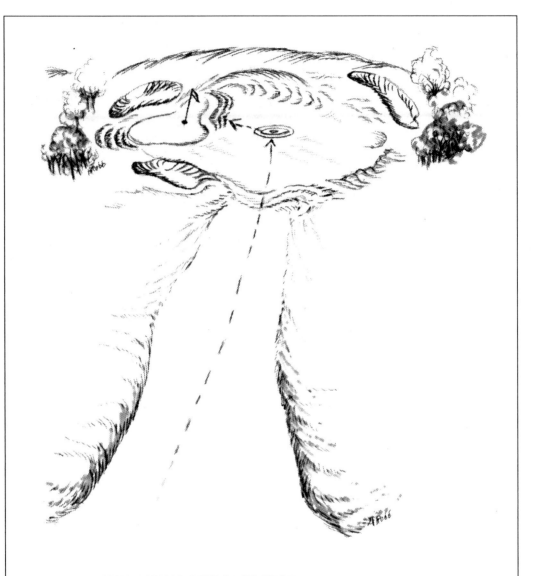

SITUATIONAL APPROACH SHOT:
The pin placement is tucked into the left front corner of a
green that slopes from back to front and slightly right -left.
The golfer is 185 yards to carry to the front of the green.

PLAN:
"SEE" the shot. The shot calls for a draw to be played off of
the target (the "fat" of the green).

INTRODUCTION

Once a golfer has developed the proper mechanics based upon an understanding of sound fundamentals, then he can really enjoy the beauty of the game. At times, the game can seem so simple (when a player is in the zone). And, at other times, it can make a person very humble.

What a game it is! To be able to see what one's potential can be and perhaps even reach it. What a thrill! Golf is a game where hard work can truly pay off. However, golfers must first learn and trust the basics of swing mechanics and develop good, solid, high-quality pre-shot and practice routines. During these routines, golfers must have and implement a solid mental process. When they do this, then they are *playing golf for the love of the game.*

It has been said that, "golf is a game that is played between the ears." How true. Once a player has developed a reasonably sound golf swing, then 80% to 90% of the game is mental. Good mental habits can be developed during practice sessions. In the Pre-**F-A-C-E**, the mental process of **F-A-C-E** was discussed and some ideas were set forth on how to use this process. This will be covered in more detail in a later chapter.

There may well be more books and articles in print on golf instruction than any other sport. Aside from the changes in golf course conditioning, the ball (it is much livelier), and technological advances in equipment, few principles in the golf swing have changed in the last 100 years. The terminology has changed, for example, pivot is now called rotation or coiling, and centeredness is now covering the ball. In *The Golf Book*, copyrighted in 1980, there is an article written by Ken Bowden in which he paraphrases the basic principles of the golf swing from writings of Harry Vardon, circa 1920. Three of Vardon's principles are included below so the reader can see how they compare to modern teachings. A more complete description of Vardon's thoughts is included in Appendix B.

The body should be easy and comfortable at address. (This principle has not changed one iota. Just watch the average golfer's practice swing. It is normally smooth and rhythmic, free of tension. Then as he addresses the ball, the golfer gets fidgety, bends over too much, spreads the feet too far apart, and in general, loses sight of the ease and comfort required of a good address position.)

Avoid straining for too wide a backswing, for if you do, you will likely sway your body. (This principle has not changed either. The last thing you want to do is over extend on the takeaway, or you will lose balance and power. When the club shaft is horizontal to the ground on the backswing, you want maximum extension with your arms but they must be comfortably extended. There should be no unnecessary stretching of your left side or arms that creates tension.)

The backswing is wound up by the swinging of the arms, the hips turning, and the left knee bending as the body pivots from the waist. (This principle is referred to as "the one-piece takeaway" in today's instruction.)

The golf swing described in the following chapters is a compilation of information that I have learned over the past 45 years of playing and teaching. The concepts and principles are the same as I teach those who come to me for instruction. These same concepts and principles can help all golfers, from beginners to professionals. *Golfing in the Zone: The Long Game* was written to provide a source for learning how to improve a golfer's thought process and visualization skills, and not as a substitute for your PGA professional's instruction. By all means, have your periodic check-ups with your PGA professional.

Because it is difficult to communicate golf swing principles in writing, you will find many illustrations throughout the book to help you better understand the concepts and principles described herein. When working with a golfer on the practice range, it may take five or more ways to point out a fault and suggest a solution for that fault before the golfer understands or relates to what is being said.

Regardless of how you play golf today, if you work on the concepts and principles contained in *Golfing in the Zone: The Long Game*, you will improve your ball striking and scoring abilities. A golfer should *not indulge in negative self-talk.* When you hit a good shot, compliment yourself, even on the practice range. *Practice with a purpose.* When visualizing shots on the practice range, (discussed in a later chapter), use positive verbal statements to reinforce your mind. This process will provide you with an awareness, through mind memory, that will carry over to the golf course when you want to hit a similar shot.

Think like a champion. When faced with a difficult shot, that is well within your skill level, use visualization and decision-making processes to —- *Focus on the moment and Commit to every shot.* Recall the times you successfully performed, similar shots. Then, go ahead and go for it.

Another important thing that champions do is keep a record or journal of their play during each round. These journals may be written or mental. For example, a golf professional recently mentioned to me that he had scored 67 in each of his last three rounds. After going over those rounds in his mind, he said he realized that his chip and run shot was weak. In those three rounds, he had executed five or six simple chip and run shots. What he found out during this review process, was that he hadn't committed to the type of chip and run shot he needed to play. He had hit the shots before he was comfortable with the club he selected or visualized where he wanted the ball to land. He used to keep a written journal of his rounds, but he has been too busy lately with his other professional responsibilities and simply didn't have the time to keep written records. These chip and run problems appeared to be more mental errors than physical ones. Had they been mechanical errors, he would have gone to the practice area and worked on his chip and run technique.

I mention this story so that the golfer/businessperson can take it to heart. If you don't already, try to review each round of golf you play and jot down the good shots and the bad ones. Determine if the bad shots were due to improper mechanics or poor judgment. Perhaps you tried to hit a shot that was beyond your capability. Maybe you hit a decent shot, but had the wrong strategy for the shot. Were you in the right frame of mind to consider the consequences of the shot? Was your mind prepared for the shot, but not your body? For example, on a rainy day, a golfer's body can tighten up without him realizing it. He might try a shot that required more flexibility than he had at the time.

Accept the ups and downs of the game. The two fundamental rules of the game are play the course as you find it and play the ball as it lies. These principles are the essence of the game. Bad lies and funny bounces happen to everyone. Take what comes and then focus on the moment. A winner has a winning attitude. The course and conditions are the same for everyone. Let your course management outshine the competition.

Keep your emotions under control. Few sports expose a player to as wide a range of emotions as does golf. Fear, anxiety, elation, anger, nervousness are just some of the feelings encountered in a round of golf. How can a golfer approach the game then? Motivational seminars normally start with goal setting and improving self-discipline. The same holds true for golf. It may be the most difficult sport in which to achieve lofty goals. Golfers are always raising the bar as they become more and more proficient. This is as it should be, because as a golfer progresses to a lower handicap, he also gains more discipline and more control over his emotions. As previously discussed, keeping a journal can help a golfer develop better methods by which to improve his thought-mechanical process. This record keeping also helps golfers: *have a positive belief in themselves and to practice with a purpose.*

Every golfer, at one time or another, has felt anger, disgust or even rage after hitting a poor shot or making a bad decision on how to play a shot. During these moments, a person's whole soul can be tested. Golf is unique in that it can reveal so much about the player. Every time a golfer tees it up, he is faced with choices. Some of those choices will lead to success and some will not. When a choice becomes a bad decision, keep in mind that there are other players in the group. Controlling emotions during these stressful times is to *show respect for others.* Remember that striking a golf ball consistently well requires a golfer to control his body and mind while maintaining a sound mechanical-thought process. Golfers should learn and remember the following Ten Commandments.

TEN COMMANDMENTS

1. Play golf for the love of the game.

2. Keep your emotions under control.

3. Focus on the moment.

4. Do not indulge in negative self-talk.

5. Think like a champion.

6. Accept the ups and downs of the game.

7. Commit to every shot.

8. Show respect for others.

9. Practice with a purpose.

10. Have a positive belief in yourself.

Posture

Without a club, set up so that you are comfortable at address. Clasp your hands together so that the palms face one another.

Posture

- Comfortable at address
- Well balanced
- Arms hanging freely
- No tension
- Back relatively straight
- Bent slightly from the waist

Extension

Avoid straining for too wide an arc on the backswing. Arms extended comfortably to obtain a one-piece takeaway.

The Backswing: Frontal View

Upper body coiled (or wound-up) over the lower body.

The Backswing: Down the line View

- Full turn of the shoulders.
- Full loading of the right side.

CHAPTER 1
UNDERSTANDING THE BASIC MECHANICS
OF THE GOLF SWING

Before focusing on the grip, stance, alignment, pre-shot routine, backswing and through-swing, it is important to understand the principles of the mechanics or physics of the golf swing in simple terms. So, let's start at the beginning.

When you were a child you may have played with a toy top. It is a common cylindrical toy that has a tapered point on which it spins. You wind it up in a clockwise twisting (rotating) motion until it won't wind up any further. There is a spring inside of it that becomes tightly coiled (storing energy). Once it reaches the maximum torsion, it will release itself (because of the energy stored up from winding it up) in an opposite rotation (counterclockwise). It spins on its axis, which is perpendicular (at a right angle) to the ground.

The golf swing uses essentially the same concept, except that it is performed on a slightly tilted axis, a sort of elliptical motion. When the top is wound up, it is basically the same as "coiling to the top" of the backswing. At the top of the backswing, a golfer's full shoulder turn gives the feeling of the upper body being coiled up like a spring. Some golfing professionals like to think of it as having their upper body coil over their lower body. The golfer should feel some resistance in the lower body, specifically in the hips (which should have turned about 45 degrees) and along the inside of the right leg and right foot, which is known as "loading" the right side.

Some modern golfers, who are considered to be power hitters, are "X-factor" hitters. The "X-factor" is defined as the difference (in degrees) of the shoulder turn when compared to the hip turn. There are golfers who try to restrict their hip turn to obtain a high "X-factor." The "X-factor" is directly related to the amount of power a golfer can generate. A person who has good flexibility in the upper torso can achieve a high "X-factor." People with shorter, heavier upper bodies should not attempt this movement, as it will create an unnatural amount of tension, resulting in poor ball striking and loss of distance. These movements are not recommended for the average golfer since they put unnecessary strain on a golfer's back due to the increased torsion that is created in the lower back area.

The through-swing in the golf swing is simply a re-rotation of the coiling (winding up) that took place on the backswing. Notice the use of the term, through-swing, in place of the word downswing. Through-swing will be used throughout this book because it signifies a swinging motion and not a hitting action. A hitting action tends to get the golfer too focused on the ball, which can create added tension during the swing. Simply using the words "hit" or "hitting" can, and in many cases does, build up tension. The average golfer and many other lower

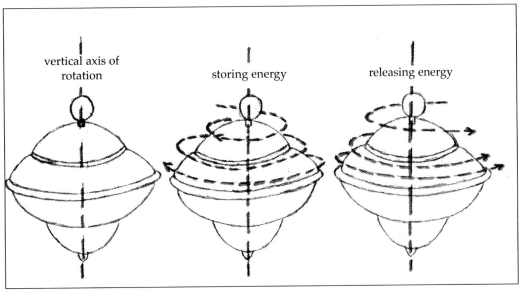

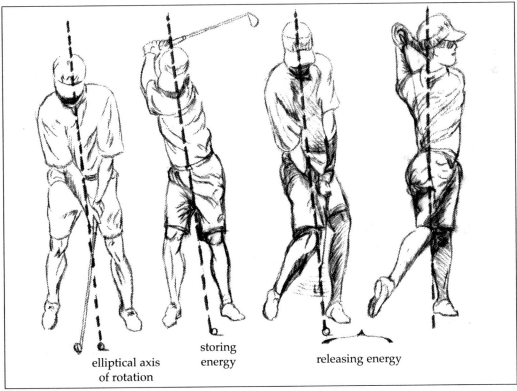

handicap players have a tendency to think about "hitting" it harder when they want to get a little extra distance. The next thing that happens is that the player is gripping the club tighter, maybe without even realizing it, while addressing the ball or during the swing. Gripping the club tighter adds extra tension in the hands and arms that decreases club head speed - just the opposite effect of what the golfer had in mind. So think about swinging the club, not "hitting" the ball. Just let the ball get in the way of a good swinging action.

Look at the following golf swing illustration and observe the points just covered. Namely, the swing taking place on a slightly tilted axis, the full shoulder turn which fully stretches the lats (latissimus dorsi), the upper body coiled over the lower body, the hips at 45 degrees, the flexed but firm position of the right leg and foot—the right side is "loaded" on the inside of the right leg and right foot.

Golf Swing — Slightly tilted axis

The golfer is set up with his spinal column tilted slightly to his right. (It is not a vertical axis as that of the toy top.)

Golf Swing — Slightly tilted axis

• Full shoulder turn around his tilted axis of rotation

• Coiled to the top of the backswing (upper body coiled over the lower body.)

• Hips are turned slightly more than 45 degrees

• Right foot, leg and hip joint are fully "loaded" and there is no sway.

Golf Swing — Slightly Tilted Axis

• At impact, he is still on a slightly tilted axis and behind the ball.

• The left arm is straight and the right arm is not.

•The left foot and leg are braced for impact. The leg still has flex, it is not rigid.

Golf Swing — Slightly Tilted Axis

At the finish, the golfer's axis or rotation is no longer tilted. He finishes on a vertical axis just like the toy top.

It sounds so simple. To have a beautiful swing with rhythm and good club head speed, all a player has to be is a toy top! Unfortunately, we are not toy tops. Ernest Jones, a great golf instructor, once said: "Golf is a simple game, it is the people who play it that make it difficult." The following basic principle of the swing is explained by a Scotsman, Tom Scott, as written in The Concise Dictionary of Golf: "take the club back as far as possible [one-piece takeaway] and then push it upwards keeping the left arm straight [relatively]. The swing should be in one movement with the aim being to bring the club head down at a speed that increases as the ball is struck. After impact, the hands should be pushed through and upwards." It does sound simple.

What should a golfer do to develop a sound golf swing? Keep it simple, like the toy top—just wind up and unwind. The following five points will help:

- Plant yourself well with your feet at address. Feel like you are digging your spikes into the ground.

- Stay planted throughout the swing. Feel as if your feet and legs are springy during the swing; the legs and feet should feel alive just like you are going to shoot a free-throw from the free-throw line in basketball.

- Work back behind the ball on the backswing. In other words, coil back behind the ball. One way to do this is to try to get your sternum over the right knee at the top of the backswing. This move ensures a full shoulder turn.

- Stay back behind the ball on the through-swing until your right shoulder (assuming you are a right handed golfer) brings your chin around and up after impact has occurred. Keep your head behind the ball until you are through the impact area.

- Let the momentum of the swing bring you to a full, well-balanced finish.

All of these points will occur if you have a properly sequenced swing from start to finish. Proper sequencing will be briefly discussed now, and then in more detail in subsequent chapters. Assuming that the golfer has the proper posture and a correct address position, the sequencing should begin with a one-piece takeaway, normally the result of some sort of a forward press that preceded it to get the swing into motion. The one-piece takeaway is generally considered to be a unified or coordinated movement of the left shoulder, left hip, left knee (turning to a point behind the ball), left foot (rolling on the instep), the left arm and hand (which extend the club head back along a path until the hands are hip high on the backswing and the clubshaft is parallel to the ground). At this point in the backswing, the shoulders continue to turn and pull the hips around with them. These actions, in turn, pull the left knee farther behind the ball and the left leg farther to the right, which shifts the weight being transferred to the inside of the right leg—from the instep up the inside of the right leg and into the inside of the right hip joint.

The sequence for the through-swing is just the reverse. The lower body initiates this part of the swing. Ben Hogan firmly believed that the turning of the hips to the left, with a slight lateral movement, initiated the downswing. Jack Nicklaus, on the other hand, felt that his feet and legs initiated the downswing.

In any event, it happens very quickly. The total time for the through-swing sequence to take place is about two-fifths of a second. Suffice it to say that the lower body – feet, legs and hips initiate the through-swing in a unified, coordinated manner. The shoulders, arms, and hands, in that order, then come into the sequence. The momentum of the swing brought about by a properly sequenced movement of body parts and the inertia of the club head will bring the golfer to a full, well-balanced finish position.

It is this unified movement of the shoulders, back, hips and legs, when coordinated with the speed of the arm and hand swing, that produces power. In other words, a golfer must use the bigger, slower muscles and the faster, smaller ones in a coordinated manner to propel the ball a long distance.

The "Planted" Golf Swing
Frame 1

- Good center of gravity.
- Relaxed and comfortable.
- "Sitting to the ball" (planted).

The "Planted" Golf Swing
Frame 2

One piece takeaway starts the swing into motion. Still planted or "sitting to the ball."

The "Planted" Golf Swing
Frame 3

- Swinging the club nicely toward the top of the backswing.
- A good wide arc with maximum extension.
- The left hip and knee are being pulled clockwise due to the arm swing.
- The left side is in complete control going back.

The "Planted" Golf Swing
Frame 4

- At the top, the golfer is fully "loaded" and has good width.
- He is still in the sitting position (planted).
- He has worked back behind the ball and is well coiled (see the wrinkles on his shirt). His sternum is over his right knee.

The "Planted" Golf Swing
Frame 5

- Starting down, he is really "pulling" and "firing."
- He is still in the sitting position and is behind the ball.
- The angles are maintained to just about belt level.
- The left side leads the through swing.

The "Planted" Golf Swing
Frame 6

- At impact, he is fully releasing the body and arms and hands.
- The left leg is properly braced and is not rigid.
- The left side has elongated.

The "Planted" Golf Swing
Frame 7

- Beyond impact, his right side has fired completely.
- The right arm is fully extended and there is good extension of both arms down the line.

The "Planted" Golf Swing
Frame 8

- The right shoulder has brought the head up and around.
- The right arm stays fully extended and the left arm is folding.
- His body rotation is still on a tilted axis.

The "Planted" Golf Swing
Frame 9

- The momentum of the swing has brought the golfer to a full, well-balanced finish, a "hoganesque" finish.

- His rotational axis is now vertical.

Accomplished players use these power sources proficiently. Average golfers use their hands and arms to swing the golf club, and basically neglect the big muscle power sources. That is not to say the arms and hands are not power sources. They move faster than any other body part used in the golf swing and therefore produce club head speed. However, they have to be coordinated with the overall sequence of the swing. On the through-swing, for example, the hips, legs and feet lead the shoulders and then the arms and hands (through the unhinging of the wrists) follow and deliver the final blow to the ball via the club head. The momentum of the swing permits the golfer to follow through to a well-balanced finish. Of course, this assumes a properly sequenced backswing has preceded the through-swing.

If this sounds too complex, think of it this way. The left side (for right-handed golfers) must lead the through-swing as it leads and controls the backswing. The better the left side is stretched or extended – comfortably – on the backswing, the more power is developed. Exactly the way the top spins at full speed.

The word "feel" is used a lot by accomplished players when they hit a good shot. What do they actually mean? Think about this. The ball is propelled by the contact made from the club head at impact. Research by Alastair Cochran and John Stobbs determined that the contact time at impact is about one-half of a thousandth of a second. It takes another two-thirds of a thousandth of a second for the shock wave to travel up the shaft to reach the hands. (The ball has already left the club face and is in flight but the hands have not yet felt the contact.) Add another ten-thousandths of a second before the "message" gets to the brain and the golfer can be said to "feel" the reaction. So by the time a golfer's hands "feel" anything, the ball is already on its way. This means that an accomplished golfer knows what a good shot feels like because of his prior experiences of hitting good shots.

Another point that Cochran and Stobbs' research showed related to the remarkable accuracy achieved by professional golfers and accomplished players in their swinging of the golf club. Accomplished players must align the club face at impact within two degrees of the direction of the swing. If they don't, they will never drive the ball within 15 yards or so of the middle of the fairway, nor strike it onto some part of the putting surface. These are pretty narrow parameters within which to confine natural human error while swinging a full-length shot. Narrow limits considering that the whole body, including a system of mechanical leverage of limbs and joints enter into the equation. They concluded that to achieve the accuracy required, the golf swing should be kept as simple as possible. Therefore, the difference between accomplished players and average golfers is the way in which they obtain full power from almost all of the muscles the human body has to utilize when swinging a golf club to propel a golf ball. The swing mechanics, thought processes, and practice drills given in the following chapters are intended to help golfers improve in all facets of their swing, resulting in lower scores.

Chapter 2
THE FUNDAMENTALS

Books, magazines, high-speed photography, photographs, videos, geometric axioms and other mathematical formulae abound on the subject of the golf swing and on the game itself. What is new or different about the swing in the past 80 years? Not a whole lot. However, it is important to cover the fundamentals of the grip, stance, posture, alignment and pre-shot routine because without these fundamentals, all golfers will struggle with their game.

Before discussing the fundamentals, I want to quote a thought about the golf swing from Arnold Haultains' book, *The Mystery of Golf,* that seems appropriate, "Someone once likened the golf swing to reading a piece of music note by note; as opposed to playing a piece of music with which you have rehearsed and are familiar. In the former example, one's brain has time to act between notes. And, in the latter example, one is playing [or swinging] by rote." My interpretation of this thought is that once golfers have developed the proper sequential movements required of a sound golf swing, then their swing can be said to be on autopilot. The brain is quiet and the physical reaction is occurring automatically.

Most golfers have experienced the brain interfering with their motion during their swing. They have felt that something just didn't feel right (grip pressure too tight, weight too much on their toes at address, etc.) and still they went ahead and made the swing, more than likely with poor results. When the brain has too much time to act, it upsets or unbalances the sequence of events, both neuronal and muscular, that must take place during the swing. The processes and procedures that follow are intended to help golfers overcome any mental and mechanical deficiencies they may currently have. For beginning golfers, these points provide a solid foundation for playing and enjoying the game of golf.

THE GRIP

Since your hands are your only contact with the golf club, it all begins with a proper grip. One of the objectives of the game is to make solid contact with the ball. Therefore, the grip needs to be firm enough to withstand the shock of impact when the club head makes contact with the ball. The firmness of the grip is to prevent twisting of the club handle in the hands at impact. On the other hand, a golfer doesn't need to have the grip pressure so tight as to tighten the muscles in the hands, wrists, and forearms. There can be no tautness of these muscles or weak shots will result. Remember that a taut muscle is a weak muscle. The proper grip is a balancing act between firmness and tenseness. It must be firm enough so that no loosening occurs at the top of the backswing, and so that there is enough grip pressure to maintain club control throughout the swing, i.e., no twisting or turning of the grip at impact.

To develop the proper grip, a golfer should grip the handle of the club with the last three fingers of the left hand. Grip the handle firmly but not tensely. The left thumb should be resting firmly on the upper right side of the club handle. Look down at your left-hand position. You should see two or three knuckles of the left hand. Then, wrap the web of the two middle fingers of the right hand around the grip handle of the club. This should put the right thumb slightly to the left side of the grip handle while the right side of the grip handle rests against the third joint pad of the right forefinger. The right thumb and forefinger form a "V" and they touch one another. Rest the "V" of the right hand against the right side of the grip handle. Also, make sure that the left thumb fits snugly into the lifeline of the right hand.

Left Hand Grip

Initially, take hold of the club with the forefinger and the muscular pad of the palm of the hand. The club handle should rest diagonally across from the base of the index finger to the base of the muscular pad. You can grip the club as shown, or, grip it in this manner while holding the club shaft vertically.

Left Hand Grip

With the last three fingers of the left hand, wrap them around the handle of the club. This should put the left thumb slightly to the right of the center as it rests against the handle. The last three fingers are the pressure points of the left hand grip.

Left Hand Grip

With the left hand firmly on the club, place the right palm in a position that faces the left hand as shown. Then, with the web of the two middle fingers of the right hand, grasp the club handle and close these two fingers around the handle.

Right Hand Grip

Once the two middle fingers are in place, then close your right thumb and forefinger on the handle. The lifeline of the right hand should fit snugly over the left thumb. And, the right thumb should be resting slightly to the left side of the handle. The right hand grip is a finger grip, that is, the web of the two middle fingers is the pressure point.

The Grip

The hands should feel as if they are molded together and work as a unit. Both "V's" point to the right of the chin. Notice the pressure point of the right thumb and forefinger where they rest against the handle. A word of caution: Do not apply too much pressure on the right thumb and forefinger as it will create tension up the right arm and into the right side. This tension can prohibit the right side from folding on the backswing.

Check points for the proper grip:

- Hold the club securely in the last three fingers of the left hand.

- Hold the club securely in the web of the two middle fingers of the right hand.

- Have the left thumb fit snugly into the lifeline of the right palm.

Additional View of the Grip

Additional View of the Grip

Holding the club vertically as shown helps to get the proper grip pressure.

There are three basic grips: The Vardon (or overlapping) grip, the baseball (or 10-finger grip), and the interlocking grip. The Vardon grip is universally used and will be the main focus of this book. It is named after Harry Vardon, who popularized it around 1896 after winning the first of his six British Opens. He didn't invent the grip, but his style of play had a major influence on its universal acceptance. It is said that his iron play was deadly accurate, so it is understandable that other golfers of his era imitated his grip. The interlocking grip seems to be the best grip for golfers who have smaller hands with short, stubby fingers. Jack Nicklaus uses the interlocking grip, and Greg Norman uses a modified version of it. By comparison, there aren't too many golfers who use the baseball grip. Regardless of which grip is used, the golfer's hands should be well on top of the club.

Harry Vardon had a lighter grip pressure than most modern golfers do, because he held the club more in his fingers. His right-hand grip was basically the same as that taught today and it molded in with his left hand. Both hands were on the club snugly so that they worked together as a unit during the swing. The "V's" pointed about halfway between his right ear and his right shoulder. In contrast, Arnold Palmer, who also uses the Vardon overlapping grip, believes that the grip is "the crucial junction point" since it must withstand the shock of impact. His hands are placed firmly on the club, but not so firmly as to create tension in the hands, wrists and forearms. His hands are close together to work as one unit. Arnold Palmer says, " There is only one way to hold the club – the right way. It may be uncomfortable at first, but you must master it to be able to play the game well."

Study the following illustrations. Review the previous material as you are studying them. What follows is a set of common points to remember whether you are a beginner, an average golfer, or an accomplished golfer. Keep the following points about the grip in mind:

- The last three fingers of the left hand are the pressure points. It is okay to feel a slight amount of tension in those three fingers and along the underside of the forearm up to the elbow. You never want to grip tight enough to create tension on the upper part of the forearm (the tensor muscle).

- The web of the middle fingers of the right hand is a pressure point.

- The pad between the right thumb and forefinger is a pressure point. This supports the club at the top of the backswing.

- As a general rule, the "V's" formed by both the left thumb and forefinger and the right thumb and forefinger at address should point to your right ear. This is known as the square position. The hands will always return to the square position at impact assuming a properly sequenced swing. Some golfers adjust their grip to play fades or draws. This author does not recommend this method of achieving fades and draws. If the "V's" point straight up to your chin, it is known as a weak grip and can cause fades or slices depending on how accomplished a player you are. This is due to the club face coming into the ball at impact in an open position because the hands would have normally returned to a square position at impact. If the "V's" point to the tip of the right shoulder, it is considered to be a strong grip that can cause hooks due to the club face being closed at impact.

- The left thumb is in the lifeline of the right hand.

- In the Vardon grip, the little finger of the right hand overlaps the forefinger of the left hand. In the interlocking grip, these fingers interlock themselves.

- The hands are close together, acting as one unit. They are holding the club firmly without creating undo tension in the hands, wrists and forearms.

Vardon Grip

The most commonly used grip.

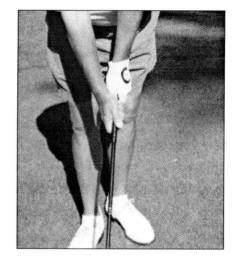

10 Finger Grip

Also known as the "Baseball Grip." Notice the slight spacing between the hands.

Interlocking Grip

This grip is used principally by golfers who have short, stubby fingers or small hands.

Square Grip — Close up view

The hands are molded together to act as one unit. The square grip provides for a proper release.

Strong Grip

"V's" point to the tip of the right shoulder. This grip can cause hooks due to a quicker releasing of the club. (The toe of the club is closed or closing at impact.)

Weak Grip

"V's" point to the left of the golfer's chin. This grip can cause slices due to a slower release (or non-release) of the club. (The face is open at impact.)

Short Thumb

For years this author used the short thumb when gripping the club. But, tenderness in the thumb forced going to the long-thumb grip. Experiment with each to determine which thumb position best suits you.

Long Thumb

Using the long thumb approach has lessened the author's grip pressure and given a better releasing action of the club.

STANCE and ADDRESS

The word "stance" is derived from the French word, "estance", meaning position; a mode of standing or being placed: posture. As it pertains to sports, it means the position of the feet of a golfer or batter preparatory to making a swing; the position of both the body and feet from which an athlete starts or operates. When looking up the word "address" in the dictionary one will find that when used as a noun it means dutiful attention to preparation. It can also be defined as a preparatory position of the player and club in golf. In golf, players are said to have "addressed the ball" when they have taken up their stance to play a shot, and have "grounded their club." In addition to helping promote the one-piece takeaway by keeping the club off of the ground at address, this definition illustrates another good reason for not soling (grounding) the club when addressing the ball. If the ball happens to move while a player is addressing it, and the player has not soled the club, then there would be no penalty assessed. If, however, the club has been soled then a penalty would occur.

The stance and address are very important starting positions for many sports. A well-balanced address position promotes a well-coordinated and balanced swing. At the very least, it will help make the swing more rhythmic and smooth, with a good tempo. The address position should always feel comfortable. Without this comfortableness, poor performance is virtually guaranteed. When using a driver, the width of a golfer's feet, as measured from the instep of one foot to the instep of the other, should be approximately the width of the golfer's shoulders. The width of the stance should become narrower as club selection progresses to the short irons. There are three positions that the feet can assume for address: **square** – both feet are parallel to the target line; **open** – the right foot is parallel and square to the target line, and the left foot is pulled back (behind) from the parallel line; and **closed** – the right foot is parallel and square to the target line, and the left foot is ahead (forward) from the parallel line.

A proper address provides for better balance during the swing. Since golfers vary in height, weight, and build, one might wonder if there is a simple method to obtain the correct posture. The answer is yes. Balance at address and during the swing is directly related to a person's center of gravity (or C.G.). The C.G. refers to one's body weight distribution at address. In simple terms, a golfer's body weight (mass) of the upper trunk should be equal to the body weight of the lower trunk. This center point varies for individuals due to their structure. For example, for short, husky people, obtaining their center of gravity may require that they have to extend their derriere out more than taller people. One simple way to check your C.G. (balance) at address is to take your address position and swing the club to the top of the backswing. Hold it. Then have a fellow golfer gently push you from behind, just above the beltline of your back. If you fall on your toes, you are out of balance. If your balance is good, you should still be in a springy position after the gentle push from behind. The center of gravity is extremely important in the address position. When golfers are centered correctly, their balance will be good and their body will not get in their way during their through-swing.

When using a driver, the left arm and club should form a straight line to the ball (which should be positioned inside the left heel). This line may be slightly ahead of the ball for medium and short irons. There are exceptions to this, however, as some accomplished golfers position their hands somewhere between their belt buckle and the inside of the left leg instead of in a straight line to the ball. This position creates a slight angle that must be compensated for at impact. The address position is a precursor for a strong impact position. And, since all good shotmakers have a straight left arm at impact, setting the arm and club shaft straight in line with the ball at address is a good way to start. A second exception is that some golfers move the ball back in their stance (to about the middle or slightly ahead of the middle of their stance) to play normal shots. In other words, they change their ball position for some normal shots. This is not the same as changing the ball position for punch shots or downhill lies, where it is advisable to do so. Look at it this way. By moving the ball back in the stance the golfer runs the risk of pushed shots, since the club is coming into the ball from the inside of the intended line and is not yet squared to the target line due to the ball being too far back in the stance. Compensation in the swing must take place to start the ball on line. Therefore, if golfers play the ball in the same relative position all of the time they minimize the angles and thus the corrections. Keep the swing as simple as possible.

Address Position — Frontal View

- Comfortable, well balanced position

- Weight equally distributed on insteps.

- Arms, shoulders, and hands are relaxed.

- Arms hang freely.

- Slightly tilted axis.

Address Position — Down the Line View

- Back is relatively straight.
- Bend is slightly from the waist.

Stance Width — 5-iron

The width of the stance, as measured from instep to instep, should be almost shoulder width.

Stance Width — Driver

The width of the stance, as measured from instep to instep, should be shoulder width.

Square Stance

Body alignment is parallel to the target line.

Open Stance

Body is aligned left of target.

Closed Stance

Body is aligned right of the target.

Straight Line at Address

The left arm and club form a straight line to the ball. The club is held off of the ground to promote a one-piece take-away.

The shoulders, hips and feet should be square and parallel to your line. The arms should hang down naturally. There should be no reaching for the ball; no crowding it. The back should be as straight as possible. There should be a slight bending forward from the waist; but do not stoop over from the shoulders. The hands should be approximately six to eight inches from your body. The legs should feel springy, but not loose. Your weight should feel evenly distributed and on the insides of both feet. Point or tuck the knees slightly inward, but do not create tension. You should be able to wiggle your toes inside your shoes.

Use the following practice drill to help check your address and balance. Take your address position and make sure that your weight is equally distributed on the inside of both feet. With a short iron, hit three-quarter shots. Let the weight on the inside of the left foot transfer to the inside of the right foot on the backswing. Be sure to use a one-piece takeaway concentrating on the rolling of the instep of the left foot. On the through-swing, during impact, make sure that the weight from the right foot is re-transferred to the inside of the left foot. It is okay to have the weight on the outside of the left foot at the finish of the swing. There should be a natural rolling of the weight to the outside of the left foot as the swing progresses to a full finish. The thrusting of the right side and the force occurring from the uncoiling will bring the weight to the outside of the left foot. At the finish, there should be very little weight on the toe of the right foot. This is the mark of a stable and well-balanced swing.

The majority of accomplished golfers use a stance that has the right foot at 90 degrees (square) and parallel to the target line. The left foot is flared out somewhere between 22 and 30 degrees to the left but still parallel to the target. Sometimes when professionals or accomplished players want to get a little more distance, especially with the driver, they flare the left foot out a little more than 30 degrees. They may also flare out their right foot to the right to get a bigger shoulder turn. The average golfer should not try this flaring out of the right foot. Ben Hogan felt very strongly about there being one correct basic stance: The right foot is at a right angle to the line of flight and the left foot is turned out a quarter of a turn to the left (about 22 degrees). In any event, the correct stance helps the proper sequencing take place on the backswing, promotes the right amount of hip turn on the backswing, and provides for the proper clearance of the hips on the through-swing. If the golfer's left foot is not flared out at address, say it is square to the line, the hip clearance through the impact area can become restricted, causing blocked shots to the right of the target and/or weak slices, commonly referred to as "wipes."

Experiment with the set-up on your own. Remember, most accomplished golfers use the left foot flare-out approach. This author has tried them all and arrived at the approach popularized by Ben Hogan as best for him. Occasionally, when a hook or hard draw is required, golfers can pull their right foot back inside the line and flare it out to the right. This set-up gets the club to the inside more quickly than normal on the backswing, which tends to produce a right to left flight of the ball. But, a word of caution, practice this move before you try it.

Setup

Left foot flared. Right knee pointed inward. Arms hanging freely. Golfer is at ease in the setup.

POSTURE

Posture, by definition, means the relative arrangements of different parts of the body; or, the position of the body (and feet) for a special purpose. Posture is very important, for without good posture in the set-up, a golfer invites unnecessary trouble and dissatisfaction while playing the game.

In order for the proper swing sequencing to occur and, consequently, to achieve a full pivot/turn on the backswing, and a fluid re-turn through the ball to a full, balanced finish, the golfer must have good posture. Without it, a golfer's body will get in the way at some point during the swing. When this occurs, a golfer will not have good ball-striking ability. Good posture demands the following:

- The arms hang comfortably from the shoulder sockets.

- The back is relatively straight.

- The waist is slightly bent.

- The knees are slightly flexed and tucked inward.

- The weight is evenly distributed between your left and right foot; and it is to the inside of each foot, i.e., on the insteps and slightly toward the heel. This helps to prevent a sway off of the ball by keeping the weight on the inside of the right foot (and the inside of the right leg) at the top of the backswing (the loading of the right side).

- Your left shoulder should be slightly higher than your right shoulder because your right hand is lower than your left hand when you grip the club. This also sets the slight tilt of the angle of the spine from the vertical at address. It also makes it easier to rotate around that tilted spine angle.

- Your left arm and club should be in a straight line to the ball.

All of these points set up a strong left side, which is essential to good ball striking. Keep in mind, the left side leads and controls the backswing. And, it leads the through-swing due to the uncoiling action, just as in the example of the top.

Posture: Frontal View

- Straight line from clubhead to the shoulder.
- Arms hanging freely from the shoulder sockets.
- Triangle is formed and relaxed.
- Weight is evenly distributed and is on the inside of both feet.
- Spinal column tilted properly.

Posture — View from Down the Line

- Back is straight.
- Butt is extended.
- Center of gravity appears to be perfect.
- Comfortable.

ALIGNMENT AND PRE-SHOT ROUTINE

Alignment is the proper positioning of parts in relation to each other. There are two types of parts that need to be aligned. Body parts are one, and the target area is the other. To play the game well, golfers must be precise in their alignment to the target. It was stated earlier that a two-degree misalignment of the face of the club at impact would cause the ball to miss the middle of the fairway by 15 yards or more with a driver. This tells you how important the alignment process is. Watch the professional tour players prior to addressing the ball. Observe them during their pre-shot and alignment routine. They are very precise. They take nothing for granted. They are not careless. They know the importance of being aligned to their target.

I have had the opportunity to practice and play a number of times with Dave Hill during the past several years. Dave, in his prime, was one of the best ball strikers on the PGA Tour. And, he can still strike it. Dave is a very nice guy with a big heart. What I appreciated most about his routine is that it never varies. His set-up is classic. After determining the type of shot that he is going to play, Dave aligns himself square to the target unless, of course, he is going to play a fade or draw. Dave always holds the club in a vertical position to the ground and in front of him. That is, he grips the club while holding it in front of him, and with the head of the club pointing toward the sky. He then has his upper arms set in place with his shoulders, and he keeps them that way throughout his swing. With his back straight, he measures to the ball by bending slightly from the waist. This sets his triangle, formed by his shoulders and arms and hands, the same every time. As he measures to the ball, he also flexes his knees and tucks the right knee inward toward the ball. This is to make sure that he gets his weight loaded onto the inside of his right leg and right hip joint on the backswing, which prevents a sway off of the ball. He wiggles his feet slightly, but firmly plants them into the ground. This is a balance check for him. His derriere is extended slightly, and his arms hang freely from his shoulder sockets. His set-up is textbook.

Set Up

- During practice, get into the habit of settling three clubs on the ground.

- Set the triangle by connecting the upper arms to the shoulder area.

Set Up

- Measured to the ball.

- Right knee tucked in.

- Firmly planted at address.

- Arms hanging freely.

Before discussing the pre-shot routine, it is important to understand what is involved. The pre-shot routine consists of two basic parts: physical and mental. The physical part encompasses:

- Aiming the club head.

- Properly aligning the body.

- Obtaining the proper posture.

- Executing the shot.

The mental part encompasses **Focus And Commitment** to the shot.

For normal shots, the club face is usually aimed square to the target. The word, "usually", is used because many accomplished players and professionals have their club face slightly open to the target at address, while a few actually have the club face closed at address. The open club face or closed club face at address is merely a peculiar trait or personal habit of these individuals.

When golfers want to hit a fade, they will sometimes open the club face slightly at address. Or, if they want to draw the ball, they may toe-in the face of the club a little. This is not a recommended procedure for the average golfer and especially for the beginner. The reason why is simply because the tendency for the less accomplished players is to align themselves in the direction the club face is aimed. This can create wild hooks or uncontrollable slices, pulls or pushes, and loss of ball control. Don't open or close the club face at address, keep it square to the target line.

The basic alignment to the target should be thought of as parallel lines, like railroad tracks. The bottom of the club face should be aimed squarely to the target. The golfer's body (feet, knees, hips and shoulders) should be parallel to the line. In other words, the club face is square to the outside railroad track, and the golfer's body is aligned square to the inside railroad track. If you want to fade the ball, the railroad tracks are parallel, and to the left of the target. If you want to draw the ball, the railroad tracks are parallel, and to the right of the target. Get into the habit of a consistent alignment procedure. Do it on the practice tee before every shot until it becomes automatic.

Alignment

To check your alignment, place two clubs on the ground as shown. The clubs are like railroad tracks. The outer rail (lighter line) represents the line on which the club is aimed. The inner rail (darker line) is the line on which your body should be aligned. This is the square set up position.

Let's walk through the pre-shot routine by way of an example. Assume that a professional tour player is preparing to play a long, par four hole, with a dogleg left. It has a forty-yard wide, firm fairway that is bunkered on the right from between 240 to 280 yards from the teeing area. Further, let's assume that during the pre-shot preparation, the golfer decides that because the hole is so long he needs to use his driver. He also decides to draw the ball off of the bunker-line, since the rough on the left side of the fairway is very punishing. See the "pre-shot routine illustration.

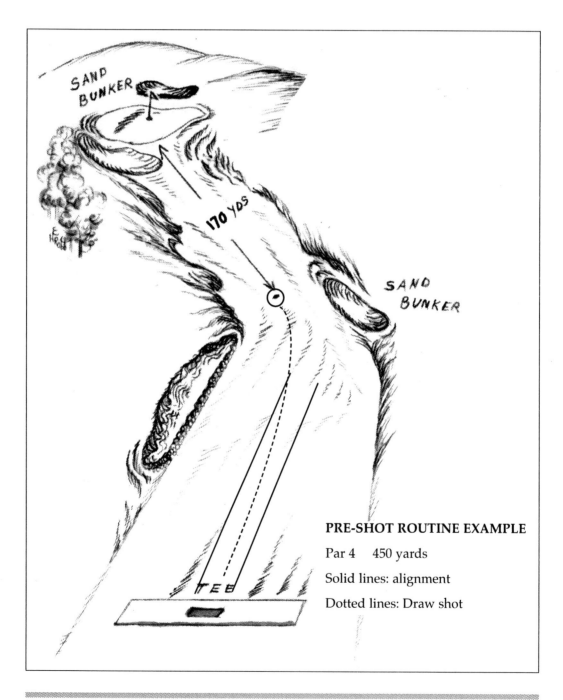

PRE-SHOT ROUTINE EXAMPLE

Par 4   450 yards

Solid lines: alignment

Dotted lines: Draw shot

The pre-shot routine brings together the mental and physical process, or as we state throughout this book, the sound thought-mechanical processes known as **F-A-C-E.** The following procedures illustrate what pre-shot routine the golfer is going to go through.

The player begins by standing directly behind and a few feet away from the ball and focuses on the target area (also known as sighting your target). This procedure helps his optical perception of the landing area, the terrain over which the ball must fly, and how far the ball will roll after landing.

Since the golfer had determined that a draw was called for, he must visualize that type of shot. In this case, a high, soft draw would be the best, and safest shot to execute because of the difficult rough on the left side of the fairway. (The run on a low, hard draw with a firm fairway would be harder to control.)

His focus on the shape of the shot must be complete. It must be intense. There can be no doubts. If there is a lot of pressure at the time and he really needs to pull off the shot, then he may recall the number of times that he has hit similar shots during a round of golf, or on the range. His focus is such that he will "see" the ball leaving the club face starting down the right side of the fairway and inside the bunker line and softly drawing into the right center of the fairway. He must then make up his mind to commit to this visual shape of the shot, as this commitment is all-important.

With this visualization and commitment in his mind, he will walk to the ball from his position behind the ball. (Some players hold the club in their right hand at this point and set the club on the ground behind the ball and line it to the target. Others hold the club in their left hand and line it to the target. Experiment to find out what technique is best for you. Remember to aim at your target using the bottom of the club face. It is important to aim carefully.)

Once his aim is set the way he wants it and he is comfortable with it, he will align his body to the target while taking his normal grip. In this case, since he wants to draw the ball, his stance would be slightly closed to the line. A slight digression is needed here. Normally, professionals have their own methods that let them know that they are aimed properly to the target, and that their stance, address, and posture are correct. All golfers have to develop their own way of knowing when they are in the proper position before they begin their swing. Go to a PGA teaching professional and work on this part of the game. It is imperative to get it right. Also, note that a number of tour caliber players pick a spot a few feet in front of the ball that is in line with the intended target. This is their way of aligning themselves to the target. They adjust their stance and body alignment parallel to that spot. At this point in the pre-shot routine, the golfer will be ready to start his swing. He must trust it and then go ahead and execute it.

These steps are as good a pre-shot routine as any. Many professional golfers use this process. Start with these basic ingredients and see if they work for you. If you have to modify the procedure, do so, but once you develop a pre-shot routine with which you are comfortable, stick with it. If for any reason you become distracted during your pre-shot routine, for example, if a maintenance truck backfires or drives by and distracts you, back off and start over. Get used to your pre-shot routine. Become dependent upon it. But be sure to make it efficient; don't let the process control you. You must control the process. After you have developed your own pre-shot routine and are comfortable with it, and after you have walked from behind the ball and addressed it, it should only be a matter of several seconds before you begin your swing. Jack Nicklaus, on the other hand, is very deliberate once he gets over the ball, and goes through a long countdown before he is ready to start his swing. Someone once asked him why it took him so long over the ball. He said, "I must get perfectly set, it is almost a compulsion, before I can pull the trigger." Please remember that we are not all like Jack Nicklaus. However, we should always take great care in our set-up, alignment, and pre-shot routine.

So, brevity and efficiency are the passwords of the day once you have taken up your address position, and have a clear picture in your mind about the type of shot that you are planning to play. When you accomplish a solid pre-shot routine and alignment procedure, it becomes easier to play the game. Without a proper approach, your results will be mediocre, at best.

In your mind, visualize the shot to be played, whether it is a high fade, or a low draw. Take into account the weather conditions, firmness of the green, how well the green is protected, the highest percentage shot, and so on. Once you have decided on the shot to be played, focus on the desired flight of the ball to get to the target area, given the conditions. This focusing must be complete. Your concentration must be total. Be intense, but not tense. Once your mind is made up, commit to it. Trust it.

Trust not only your mental process, but your mechanical process as well. This is what commitment really is, trusting oneself to perform as planned. There can be no doubt. You have rehearsed and successfully completed enough shots at the practice range and from other rounds of golf, to trust your swing and your mental process. The **Focus And Commit** stages bring about the **Execution** stage. This is the final piece of the sound thought-mechanical process. This is the application of the principles of **F-A-C-E**.

There can be no doubts during the procedure. Trust your thought-mechanical process, and go ahead and execute the shot. If you are able to visualize good shots, the likelihood of them happening is much greater. The more acutely you "see" the shot, the more likely the success. Think success, not failure. You must exercise good discipline not only to develop your pre-shot routine, but also to stick with it no matter how poorly you may be playing on any single day.

Pre-shot Routine

- Stand eight to 10 feet directly behind the ball.
- Focus on the shape of the shot to be played to the landing area.

Pre-shot Routine

- Approaching the ball.
- Committing to the shape of the shot.

Pre-shot Routine

- Setting up to execute the shot. (Set up appears to be open. Golfer is playing a fade to the landing area.)
- Taking one last look at the landing area before triggering the swing.

BALL POSITION

The position of the ball is vital since the objective of good ball striking is to make square contact with the ball time after time. The ball position may vary slightly for each individual, but, for almost all accomplished golfers, the ball is positioned to the inside of the left heel. This is the point at the bottom of the golfer's swing where the club head is traveling along the intended line of flight. That is, the club head has come from inside of the line to the square position. And, it is aimed down the intended line before it starts back to the inside of the line again. For the driver, this point should be at the bottom of the swing or slightly past the bottom. You may have heard the expression " hit it on the upswing." This implies that a golfer contacts the ball slightly past the bottom of his swing in order to reduce the underspin on the ball. Consequently, the ball will roll farther when it hits the ground. If the ball is too far back in your stance and you are swinging properly, i.e., from the inside to square to inside, then a pushed shot, or a blocked shot would result due to the club face being open to the line at impact. Conversely, if the ball is positioned too far forward, and you are swinging properly, then a pulled shot or pull hook would result due to the club face being closed to the target line.

Golfers should determine where their swings "bottom out" for the driver and other clubs. A good exercise is to swing at the tip of the grass or a weed and notice where your club bottomed out. Or, place a tee in the ground and observe where the club head is when contact is made. (Incidentally, have you ever noticed how well a golfer swings at a weed? The swing is usually smooth with good tempo. There is no ball there to tighten his muscles. Nor, is there a target to hit.) Golfers must determine where the bottom of their swing is – the point at which the club face is square to the target line during the through-swing – for the correct ball positioning. You may find out that your swing dictates that your ball position may be okay off of the left heel for the driver, but you may need to move the ball toward the middle of your stance for shorter shots. Experiment using the trial and error method, or consult your PGA Professional, to find out where your optimum ball positioning is for normal shots. Then, stick with it.

Ball Positioning — Driver

Play the ball off of the left instep. Notice that the left foot is flared slightly.

Ball Positioning — 5-iron

Play the ball off of the left instep.

Ball Positioning — Wedge

Play the ball off of the left instep and narrow the stance. (Many accomplished golfers open their stance when playing wedge shots.)

Ball Positioning — 5-iron

Some golfers move the ball back in their stance slightly as they progress from the driver to the shorter irons. Each golfer should experiment to find his optimum ball position for the irons.

Ball Positioning — Wedge

Ball in the middle of the stance.

THE SWING

The following illustrations show the sequencing that takes place in a well-coordinated and balanced swing with the driver. Look at them closely and note the following points:

Frame 1.   A comfortable and relaxed address position with good stance width providing a solid foundation.

Frame 2.   The "waggle" to rehearse the path of the swing.

Frame 3.   A one-piece takeaway with good extension and a stretching of the left side comfortably.

Frame 4.   The continuing turn of the shoulders and arm swing is pulling the hips farther around to the left.

Frame 5.   At the top of the backswing, the golfer has fully loaded the right side with no sway. He has coiled his upper body over the lower body (note the wrinkles in his shirt). Maximum tension in these muscles produces maximum speed, which produces distance.

Frame 6.   The hips and legs initiate the through-swing and the angles are maintained. The golfer is "pulling" nicely with the left arm.

Frames 7 & 8. The golfer is "firing" the right side into a well-braced left side. The club is being released through the ball. The arms are fully extended down the line.

Frame 9.   The momentum of his swing is carrying him to a fully extended follow through that is well-coordinated and balanced.

It is this well-coordinated swing sequence which provides the power that will be discussed later in this book.

Learn and understand the basic swing sequence. Once you do, you will be well on your way to playing good, solid golf. There is also an added bonus, since you will also learn how to monitor your swing and be able to correct any deficiencies that may occur from time to time.

The proper set-up, address and alignment coupled with a one-piece takeaway and coordinated (sequenced) movement of body parts on the backswing, make the through-swing automatic — a reflexive or reactive return of what previously took place.

**Swing Sequence
Frame 1**

Comfortable address position. Wide stance for solid foundation.

**Swing Sequence
Frame 2**

The "waggle" to rehearse the path of the swing.

**Swing Sequence
Frame 3**

One-piece takeaway gets the swing into motion.

**Swing Sequence
Frame 4**

Good, wide arc. The shoulder turn and arm swing are pulling the hips around to the golfer's right (clockwise).

**Swing Sequence
Frame 5**

At the top of the backswing, he is fully "loaded." The club is set well and is square to the line. Note how he is still in the "sitting" position.

**Swing Sequence
Frame 6**

The hips and legs initiate the through-swing dropping the club "into the slot." He is "pulling" nicely with the left arm and the set angle is maintained. Look at how well he is "sitting to the ball."

**Swing Sequence
Frame 7**

"Braced" and "firing." A very powerful position.

**Swing Sequence
Frame 8**

Fully cleared and extended through the ball. Left side is elongated.

**Swing Sequence
Frame 9**

The finish is the result of a well-balanced, coordinated swing.

Technically speaking, from set up to impact and beyond and into a full, well-balanced finish, this is a swing for all golfers to emulate.

SEQUENCE OF THE BACKSWING.

In Chapter One, I discussed the way the body parts moved to coil back behind the ball on the backswing. It is almost universally agreed that the first 12 to 24 inches away from the ball is the most critical movement in the development of a well-coiled backswing. It builds up the proper tension in the muscles of the body, and consequently, stores energy for release at impact. This first movement sets the tone of the swing. If a golfer takes the club away in a jerky motion, it is quite likely that the sequence will not occur in the proper fashion. Likewise, if the club is snatched away with the hands, the swing is destined for failure. The one-piece takeaway is the way in which the majority of professionals and accomplished players have patterned their backswings' first move. Many times, however, the movement is started with a forward press of some sort. So before we discuss the one-piece movement, let's talk about the forward press and its purpose.

The forward press is both a tension reliever and a swing starter. Many well-known players including Sam Snead, Gary Player, John Mahaffey, Billy Casper, Sergio Garcia, V.J. Singh, and David Duval, use a forward press. It is usually performed with a slight move to the left with the right knee and the right hand pushing to the left in a simultaneous motion. This movement gets the lower body into a slight forward motion allowing the golfer to establish a recoiling action, which initiates the one-piece takeaway. This recoiling motion into a one-piece takeaway insures that the hips will wind up (and not sway) on the backswing – an essential ingredient for turning back behind the ball.

If you do not use the forward press to relieve tension and start the backswing, then try the "waggle." Or, try to do what Jack Nicklaus does. He starts his backswing with a turning of his chin to the right. Some players keep the club head off of the ground, and find that this helps to start the club away in a more relaxed manner and in a one-piece fashion. If the backswing is started properly and the hips have a full wind up, with respect to the upper torso, then the through-swing has a higher probability of being a swing with full power, rather than a hitting or lunging action.

Ben Hogan felt very strongly about the waggle. He viewed it as the bridge between the address and the start of the backswing. He also felt that it was to be used as a preview of the backswing, as well as a tension reliever. In his mind, the waggle provided a synchronicity to the rhythm for the desired swing. The waggle consists of a slight break of the left wrist through the movement of the fingers of the left hand. There is arm and club movement as well. There is also a little foot movement, which is intended to provide additional feel for the shot to be played. The waggle helps to get the club started on the proper swing path for the backswing. Please refer to Ben Hogan's Five Fundamentals of Golf for a more detailed accounting of the waggle. Karrie Webb, an LPGA touring professional, has a swing preview that is an adaptation of the waggle. She takes about a three-quarter slow, one-piece rehearsal of the backswing. You should experiment with the forward press, the waggle, the turning of the chin to the right or try some adaptation of these movements to get the swing underway. Personally, I have found out through trial and error that the forward press of the right knee kick helps to get my swing sequence started in the right fashion.

The one-piece takeaway is a coordinated movement of the left side of the body and the club until the club shaft and left arm are parallel to the ground on the backswing. The club should start back straight from the ball "low and slow" with the maximum extension of the club and both arms that is comfortable. The club head will start back along the line for about a foot or so and then it will turn inside the line because of your shoulders and hips turning/pivoting to the right/clockwise. This unified movement of the left shoulder, hip, knee, foot, left arm and hand extend the club head along this path until approximately hip high on the backswing. From this point on the swing is in motion. The shoulders continue to turn and the arms are swinging the club up to the top of the backswing. The motion actually pulls the hips to their proper full turn (about 45 degrees). The continuing of the shoulder turn and arms swinging the club to the top of the backswing, allows the left foot to roll farther to the right on its instep and allows the left knee to break behind the ball farther. This, in turn, transfers weight from the left side to the right side. This weight transfer must be supported along the inside of the right foot, leg and hip joint — the loading of the right side. This is the principle reason for tucking the right knee in at address. If the weight transfer moves the right foot to the outside on the backswing, it is known as a sway off of the ball. It forces one to make a correction for it during the downswing, which is extremely difficult to do. The normal problem is that you can't get the club head back to the proper position at impact because your body position isn't where it is supposed to be.

Many average golfers think that they take the club away in a one-piece manner. But upon closer examination, they actually use their hands too much at the start of the takeaway, thus causing them to pick the club up too quickly and set their wrists too soon. This produces a shorter arc on the backswing, and usually results in a jerky and untimed swing, causing loss of distance and control. The longer the arc or the greater the extension, the farther you will drive the ball.

Address

Just before pulling the trigger with a forward press.

Forward Press

Right knee "kick" to the left to start the swing. Note that there is a slight lower body rotation to the golfer's left. The forward press allows the golfer to recoil and just let the back-swing happen.

Waggle

A tension reliever and a preview of the club path going back.

Waggle Adaptation

A rehearsal of the swing path. Karrie Webb does something similar to this before each shot.

EXTENSION AND WIDTH

In the preceding illustrations, particularly frames three, four, and eight, you can see the full extension of not only the backswing but also the full arm extension during the through-swing. As previously stated, distance or power is derived from maximum extension or a longer arc on the backswing. It is vital to understand that the extension going back must be a comfortable stretching. Do not try to extend too far back, as it will cause a sway, which can ruin a good golf swing. When the golfer executes a one-piece takeaway and has achieved maximum extension, the club shaft should be parallel to the ground with the club face square to the line. It is at this point in the backswing that the club starts to travel inside the line and is swung upwards. Your set-up and one-piece takeaway has essentially determined how well the ball will be struck. It is also at this juncture that the shoulders continue their turn and pull the hips more to the right to get them loaded, along with the right foot and leg. A good, completed backswing stretches the muscles between the hips and the upper torso. These stretched muscles create tension in both the upper torso and the lower body. This tension is the source of the big muscle power (just as the toy top was wound up.) As the hands and arm are being swung upwards, the stretching and the weight of the club head will set the club at the top of the backswing by the cocking of the wrists.

Average golfers, as well as many accomplished players, get into trouble at this point in their swing. While they may obtain a good extension, they do not complete their shoulder turn, and just pick the club up with their hands and arms. This movement shortens the arc, throws the timing off and causes weak shots, such as pushes, blocks, or even pop-ups due to the swing being too vertical. What essentially happens is that the upper-body coiling power is lost. The lower body is likely to sway, because the weight does not stay on the inside of the right foot, leg, and hip joint.

It is necessary at this point to define another term – width. Width, for the purposes of this discussion, is the distance of the hands from the right shoulder at the top of the backswing. The hands should be at their maximum width from the right shoulder if the proper coiling has taken place. Frame five shows the proper coiling. (Notice the wrinkles in the golfer's shirt.) This is a very professional position. The beginner should try to set the club at the top with a natural wrist cock that occurs from the swinging of the club to the top of the backswing. Notice that in frame five, the golfer has maximum width. Average golfers get into trouble with their width. The tendency is to allow the hands to "collapse" toward the shoulder at the top of the backswing. This loss of width also causes loss of power and usually makes the swing become too much of a hand swing.

Extend back from a one-piece takeaway. This motion should be a result of the recoiling action of the forward press and should occur in a slow, smooth rhythmic movement. Think s-l-o-o-o-w. Avoid fast, jerky motions. Let the bigger, slower muscles have time to do their job. Let the comfortable arm extension on the backswing start the coiling of the muscles between the upper torso and the hips and legs. Swing the club up to the top while continuing to turn the shoulders. Load the right side and allow the club to set at the top. These moves will put the golfer into a strong position for the "pulling" and "firing" on the through-swing.

If all of the proper sequencing has taken place, the grip pressure is correct, and the set-up is proper, then the golfer will have control of the club at the top of the backswing. It is how the golfer gets to the top that is important. It will not happen on its own. A full and complete backswing is the result of being able to work back behind the ball – to get your back to face the target and get at least a 45 degree hip turn.

Extension

One-piece takeaway with comfortable extension.

- The left arm, shoulder and lats are pushing the club away. The club shaft is almost parallel to the ground and the arms are comfortably extended.

- The let hip is beginning to be pulled to the right and the left knee is breaking to the left.

Extension

Down the line view.

Width

Width at the top of the backswing is defined as the distance the hands are from the right shoulder. Keeping your width gives you a better arc and prevents collapsing the arms at the top.

Square at the Top

The left wrist and arm are in a straight line. The club shaft is parallel to the target line.

Open at the Top

The left wrist is "cupped" as shown. The club is pointing to the right of the target line, which is also known as "crossing the line."

Closed at the Top

The left wrist is "bowed" as shown. The club is "layed-off" (to the left) of the target line.

THE THROUGH-SWING

The term through-swing is being used rather than downswing because downswing implies that there was an upswing as opposed to a backswing. If we think "back and through," it gives the mental impression of a swing. Kind of like how a pendulum works – back and through with a smooth rhythm and tempo. Downswing also implies a downward hitting action at the ball, or that perhaps we should be finishing our swing with an upswing. This would mean that there would be three parts to a golf swing: the backswing, the downswing, and the upswing. This would get too confusing and ridiculous. We are talking about developing a full, unhurried swing to a full, well-balanced finish. Swinging, not hitting. The swing is the thing.

A free swing lacks tension. Tension prohibits relaxation. A hitting action, especially hitting at the ball in a downswing, increases anxiety. The grip pressure can get tighter and tighter. The muscles can become taut causing a less forceful blow to the ball at impact; which is the opposite of what the golfer desires. A free swing, on the other hand, increases the probability of applying the proper force to the ball through impact. The term "through impact" favors a swinging action as opposed to a hitting action or muscling the ball. That is the rationale for using the term through-swing.

So far, the sequence of the backswing has unfolded. If it has been properly sequenced, then the through-swing should be a re-rotation or re-turn of the sequence opposite to the way it was developed on the backswing. To say it another way, the through-swing is a re-coiling of the stored up energy built up on the backswing. It is a reflexive action of what preceded it. The muscles should be so stretched that to try and hold the position at the top could cause some strain.

The through-swing takes place in about two-fifths of a second. It begins with a lower body movement. Nicklaus feels that he slams his left foot to the ground which simultaneously begins the re-transfer of his weight from the inside of the right foot, leg and hip joint to the inside of his left foot. By pushing hard off of the right foot he "fired" his right side. Whereas, Hogan felt that his hip re-rotation (with a slight lateral movement) began his through-swing sequence. The hands and arms should feel as if they are still at the top of the backswing, even though they have dropped down about a foot or more because of the lower-body initiation of the through-swing. Hogan's lower body move dropped his hands down to a level almost hip high – commonly referred to as the hitting area. He also felt that the hips were the most critical element to the downswing. And, if they were turned to the left properly, they released the other body parts in a cohesive movement that maximized their stored energy.

Once the through-swing sequence has begun, due to the lower-body initiating move, the shoulders, arms and hands will follow in that order. Each of these power sources releases their stored up energy to provide a powerful blow to the ball. This sequential move has been referred to as a chain reaction that continually turns on the power by increasing the speed at which the club head travels toward the ball and beyond impact. As the through-swing is completed, the hips should have rotated completely and the hips and belt buckle should face slightly left of the target. They should be level at the finish.

The shoulders re-turn in an opposite fashion to the way they turned on the backswing, and catch up to the hips at the finish. The right shoulder moves down and under the chin and brings it and the head up and around at the finish. Just before and during impact the left shoulder moves up and back. It is this move that provides the upward thrust of the left side, i.e., left shoulder, left lats, left hip and firm but flexed left leg with the weight still on the left instep. Some teachers refer to this as hitting into a firm brace. A good drill for practicing this motion is to have a person kneel behind you while you make a swing, and during impact, have them grab your left rear pocket and pull it back and to the right.

The arms and hands follow the shoulders in the sequence with a "pulling" action of the left arm. This "pulling" action brings the right elbow in close to the right hip with the wrists still cocked and loaded ready to release. By this time in the through-swing the hands and arms have dropped down to about hip high, also known as "dropping into the slot." Simultaneously, the right knee and foot are "firing" through the ball. If a golfer allows his hands and arms or shoulders to start the through-swing, as many average golfers invariably do, the chance of a good shot is virtually nil. The hip rotation is restricted and the upper body gets in the way of the swing. The swing becomes an arm and shoulder swing, most likely from outside the line, causing a slice or a pull. In any event, a poor shot results. The power derived from the big muscles of the back and legs are diminished considerably. A slower body rotation speed results. This prohibits the "pulling" and "firing" action, thereby reducing power, accuracy, and solid contact.

Now the club is ready to be released through the uncocking of the wrists and counter-clockwise rotation of the forearms. The back of the left hand should be square to the target at impact. Hogan referred to this as supination of the left wristbone, i.e., the left wristbone is being raised slightly and pointing toward the target. The right arm is not yet fully extended. It becomes fully extended about 10 thousandths of a second after the club has impacted the ball. Actually, the club head reaches its maximum speed after impact when both arms are extended. About halfway into the finish, the left arm begins to fold (about hip high) just as the right arm did on the backswing. The right arm continues to the finish and ends up in a relatively straight position.

The left foot should support almost all of the weight at the finish. The right foot should only have the toe on the ground. One very good drill to see if you are swinging in balance is to "walk-through" at the finish. If you have swung the club in balance, you should be able to take a step forward toward your target with your right foot. Gary Player has done this throughout his career.

The left side, if properly stretched or wound up on the backswing, will be in control during the through-swing so that the "pulling" and "firing" can occur. It allows the through-swing to be a swinging motion, not a hitting action. One other note, the "pulling" and "firing" cannot happen unless the golfer works back behind the ball on the backswing.

Let's address the "pulling" and "firing" action. To do so, we must backup to the beginning. The address position must be free of unnecessary tension. The hands cannot be too tight on the club. There can be some tension on the underneath side of the forearms, but not along the tensor muscles on the top of the forearms. The triangle formed by the shoulders, arms and hands should be free of tension, but not too loose. Finally, the right side must be "soft" at address so that it can "fold" more easily on the backswing. In other words, you have to get the right side out of the way going back to achieve a full turn. And, you have to get the left side out of the way on the through-swing so that your arms have room to swing freely through the impact area and beyond. The right arm and right shoulder must be as relaxed as you can get them at address; and they must stay as relaxed as they can during the backswing.

If you reach for the ball, tension creeps into the right hand and right side. When this occurs, it can not only inhibit the full turn required on the backswing, but can cause you to pick the club up about halfway back. This is known as having "lift" in the swing; not a desirable technique to have as it results in a loss of power and distance control with your iron play. And, since it gives the golfer a false turn, the golfer won't know when he is at the top of the swing because the sequence has been upset.

The left side controls the backswing through its coiling or stretching motion. It also leads the right side during the through-swing. The "pulling" and "firing" movements happen virtually simultaneously with the initiation of the lower-body move to begin the downswing. Remember that we are talking about the whole through-swing taking place in two-fifths of a second. The hips turning counterclockwise from the top of the backswing cause the golfer to drop the hands and arms into the hitting area and begin the transfer of weight from the inside of the right foot, knee, leg and hip joint to the inside of the left foot. The "pulling" of the left arm is taking place as the hands and arms are descending. The feeling should be as if you are going to swing a tennis racket to hit a back-handed topspin shot, or as if you are swinging the club with the left arm only. Many tour professionals refer to this "pulling" downward with the left arm as "tolling the bell."

Simultaneously, the right knee is "firing" to a point in front of the ball. The knee will face the target after impact occurs. This action is known as pushing off of the right side or "firing" it. This "firing" action depends on the right side being relaxed at address and during the backswing. The right side has to "fold" easily so that it can be loaded as a result of the transfer of weight from the left side to the inside of the right side on the backswing. In this way, maximum power can be delivered from the big, relaxed muscles of the body.

IMPACT POSITION

For the impact position, refer to the illustration of Ben Hogan. This impact position is "as good as it gets." He could not be in this position if any of the preceding moves were out of sequence. Study this illustration while observing the following:

The head position. His head is behind the ball and waiting for the right shoulder to bring it up and around to a finish position.

The shoulders. The left shoulder is moving up and back while the right side is "firing." The left side has completely led the through-swing. Look at the right shoulder being down and under.

The hips. The hips have cleared, i.e., moved well past the their position at address. They are looking at or facing the target. It is important to continue the hip rotation to arrive at a full, well-balanced finish. The hips and back are the two greatest power sources a golfer has. To use one or both of them ineffectively reduces a golfer's capability to get adequate distance, control and accuracy. These are the very things for which proficient golfers strive. This position allows the arms and hands to swing freely and pour on their power. Notice the straight left arm at and through impact. The right arm has not yet been fully extended. This is another checkpoint that the left side has led the through-swing.

The legs. The left leg is braced for impact. Notice that the left leg is still flexed and not rigid. If the left leg got too rigid or in a locked position before the hips have cleared, the hips will become restricted and stop their rotation. This could cause a blocked shot to the right. It could even cause a hook if the right arm took over too soon and overpowered the left arm. There is virtually no chance for anything bad to happen in this illustrated swing.

The left foot. Notice the position of the left foot. The weight is still on the inside of the left foot braced for the delivery of the club head's blow to the ball. The weight doesn't get to the outside of the left foot until he is at the finish of the swing.

The right knee and foot. The right knee is pointing past the original ball position and almost pointing to the target (the ball is on its way). The right foot has rolled to the left and the right heel is coming off of the ground. This is really "firing" the right side. Look at the right hip thrusting forward through the ball.

The arms. As noted above, the left arm is straight at and through impact while the right arm is beginning to straighten. The right arm straightens just a shade before the arms reach hip high on the follow-through.

The hands. At impact, the hands are either in line with, or slightly ahead of the club head. The back of the left hand and wrist is slightly bowed outward. Hogan referred to this as a supination of the left wrist through impact. Supination helps golfers get the same or similar ball flight (trajectory) on their shots, thereby providing for better distance control. If the left wrist were to collapse at this point, as happens to many average golfers, the tendency would be to "balloon" the ball, which leads to inconsistent ball flight and erratic distance control. Notice that both hands are pouring on the power, although the right hand seems to be really pouring it on. (I remember one time when taking a lesson from Ben Doyle, a "golfing machine" devotee, he said, "at impact use the right hand and 'drive it to China'." Translation: power the ball at impact with the right hand.)

Finally, notice the "upward thrust" of the left side during the bracing action. This elongation of the left side is the most powerful move in the golf swing. And, it requires practice to achieve it.

What can a golfer do to emulate this position at impact? Start with the proper grip. Then work hard to develop the proper set-up, posture (obtain the right C.G.), alignment, and pre-shot routine; also work on the fundamentals of the one-piece takeaway and a full turn on the backswing. If a golfer can work hard to get the right sequence starting the backswing, he has a better chance to get the right sequence for the through-swing, and therefore, get into a reasonably good impact position.

Of course we cannot all look like Hogan does in this illustration. But by practicing the basics of the swing with a good observer, perhaps your PGA professional, you can go a long way towards achieving a better and more efficient swing that will engage the proper sequencing.

Understand and believe in these principles and with a lot of practice and patience, you will be on your way to having your own game be "as good as it gets."

Reprinted with the permission of Historic Golf Prints.

THROUGH-SWING SUMMARY

In summary, it is difficult to explain the through-swing better than Ben Hogan did in his book *Five Lessons- The Modern Fundamentals of Golf.* To paraphrase what he said: The downswing begins with a turning of the hips back to the left. This movement of the hips automatically lowers the arms and hands to a position just above the level of the hips. In a chain action of the downswing, the hips are the pivotal element. The turning of the hips to the left releases the body, legs and arms in a cohesive movement to the left. In this chain action, the shoulders and the upper part of the body conduct the multiplying power into the arms. The arms multiply it again and pass it on to the hands. The hands multiply it in turn by releasing the wrists. As a result the club head is simply tearing through the air at an incredible speed. (Therefore, if the big muscles control the backswing, they should automatically control the through-swing. The "pulling" and "firing" effect is a result of a properly sequenced backswing that has stored energy, and a properly initiated through-swing that releases the stored energy.)

When you practice, get into the habit of working on one swing thought at a time. For example, once you are satisfied that you have achieved the proper sequential moves reasonably well, think about "pulling" from the top on one swing. On the next swing, think about "firing" the right side. Once your efficiency improves in these mechanical areas, you will be ready to implement visualization into your practice sessions through the principles of **F-A-C-E**.

Remember the golf swing is a development of muscle and neuronal memory. The better you wind up, the easier it is to unwind and strike the ball with power. The more you do it, the more memory you build up in the muscular and neuronal networks. When faced with a pressure situation, it is the brain memory that will bail you out. Try to adapt the following into your practice sessions and into your golf course management:

- See it,
- **F-A-C-E** it, and
- Trust it.

What provides the power seen in the impact illustration of Ben Hogan is club head speed at impact. In mathematical terms, it is the mass of the club head times how fast it was traveling at and through impact, ($F = MxA$). A golfer must not only swing the club and rotate the body around an axis, but the movements must be well timed. When the body rotation is sequenced properly, and is coupled (or timed) with the speed of the arm swing, then the golfer should be delivering maximum club head speed to the ball. Stated another way, when the lower body movement (complete sequenced body rotation) including the "pulling" and "firing" action is coupled with the speed of the arms and hands (uncocking of the wrists) on the through-swing, then, and only then, can the golfer deliver the full amount of stored energy (energy that was built up on the backswing) to the ball through the impact area.

The rotation of the body and the arm swing is the way proficient golfers "release" through the ball. This "release" is not just a release of the body through rotation but also a release of the arms and hands which in turn release the club head. The forearms actually rotate clockwise on the backswing and counter-clockwise on the though-swing. The hands apply their power through the uncocking of the wrists. Some golfers preset their forearms clockwise at address to achieve better arm rotation.

The momentum produced by the body rotation and the arm swing during the through-swing pulls the golfer up and around to a full, well-balanced finish. The golfer builds up energy on the backswing. He activates the through-swing through a unified and coordinated lower body rotation. This movement allows the upper trunk and the club head to lag the lower body movement. And, it helps to maintain balance throughout the swing. The thrusting of the right side, the continuing rotation of the body, and the inertia of the club head combine to bring the golfer to his follow-through position.

At the finish or follow-through, almost all of the golfer's weight should be on, and toward the outside of the left foot. The right foot should have only the toe on the ground. The golfer's body should be facing the target. The balance should be perfect, with the golfer having the feeling of being in a stable position. He should be able to hold himself in that position. A good habit to develop when you are at the practice range is to hold your finish on every shot until you see the ball hit the ground.

One more term to discuss is the swing plane. Ben Hogan spent several pages talking about it in his *Five Fundamentals of Golf*. So did Jack Nicklaus in his book *Golf My Way*. Hogan's illustrations were very good. He used an illustration of a sheet of glass that rested on his shoulders and was inclined upwards from the ball. The sheet of glass had a hole in it so that he could put his head through it. The idea was that the backswing would stay under this sheet of glass; and so would the downswing. For those of you interested in reading about what the swing plane is, please refer to the aforementioned books.

I believe that if golfers set up to the ball properly, as outlined in this book, and have their center of gravity established, and follow the sequencing movement previously discussed, they will swing in the proper plane. I say this regardless of the golfer's build. Obviously, taller golfers would have a more upright swing plane; shorter, huskier players would have a flatter swing plane. Nicklaus' swing plane, by design, was very upright, while Hogan's was quite flat.

The following are some points to remember after beginning the swing with a forward press.

- Strive for a one-piece takeaway.

- Roll the left instep, to the right.

- Never let the weight get to the outside of the right foot on the back swing.

- Never let the right knee lock on the backswing.

- Keep the head behind the ball. Keeping it steady is best. It should not "bob" up and down.

- Return the hips to the left to start the through-swing.

- "Pull" the left arm toward the ball.

- "Fire" the right knee toward the target.

- Let the hands lead the club head into the impact area.

- Keep the left knee flexed (not rigid) during impact. The left knee should be pointing left of the target.

- Let the left side thrust upward during impact.

- Continue the rotation of the hips and shoulders all the way to a full, well-balanced finish.

Full Swing Sequence

Good posture and well-balanced set-up.

Full Swing Sequence

Good extension with an earlier pre-set than most professionals.

Full Swing Sequence

- At the top, the golfer has worked behind the ball.

- The right side is "loaded".

- There is good width.

- The golfer has over a 100- degree shoulder turn.

- The hip turn appears to be less than 45 degrees.

- This is an "x-factor" swing.

Full Swing Sequence

The hips and lower body "bump" creates the "drop" action of the club.

Full Swing Sequence

The "pulling" and "firing" actions are taking place. The angles are maintained.

Full Swing Sequence "Bracing" for impact.

- The left side is elongating.
- The right side is "firing".
- Notice the flex in the left knee.
- The left arm is straight.
- This hips are clearing.

Full Swing Sequence Follow-Through

- Halfway into the finish the weight is starting to get to the outside of the left foot.
- The arms have extended well down the target line and are fully released.
- The head is being released.

Full Swing Sequence Finish

- The momentum of the swing brings the golfer to a full finish position.
- The right foot has very little weight on it.
- The golfer is well-balanced and facing the target.
- From this balanced position. The golfer could easily take a step forward and "walk-through" toward the target.

CHAPTER 3
"FEEL HOW THE BODY PARTS WORK"

In the preceding chapters, we discussed in some detail the set up, posture, alignment, pulling and firing and how to trigger the swing. The sequencing of the swing was also described in depth. Understanding how the body works during the swing is essential for being able to correct swing deficiencies as they arise. In this chapter, we are going to discuss how each of the body parts react during the swing, provide you with a process to monitor these "feelings" and determine if they are working as they should be.

THE HEAD. The head should be bent just enough to see the ball and yet far enough back so that it doesn't have to be moved out of the way by the left shoulder on the backswing. The chin should not be tucked into the chest. At the top of the backswing, the chin should almost rest on the left shoulder. When the left shoulder gets under your chin, then you know that you have completed the backswing.

Try to keep the head stationary throughout the swing. Some movement of the head to the right on the backswing (for right-handed golfers) is acceptable. Jack Nicklaus cocks his head to the right to start his backswing. It looks like he sets his head on his right shoulder. Do not move the head up and down or mis-hits will result. Get your head behind the ball and leave it there through impact. The right shoulder will bring it up and around as your body rotation completes itself at the finish of the swing. In the proper address position, where the shoulders and upper trunk have a slight right tilt to them, the head should be positioned slightly to the right of the ball.

Many great golfers including Arnold Palmer, Jack Nicklaus, and Ben Hogan believe that keeping the head very steady, if not absolutely still, throughout the swing is the most important fundamental of the golf swing. These great players are adamant about this. In fact, Nicklaus stated that the principle reason for the quiet head was: "The head, or at least the neck or the top of the spine, is the fulcrum or hub of the swing. As such, any shifting of it up, down or sideways must inhibit or weaken the spring-like coiling of the body on the backswing that is so essential to the generation of proper leverage on the forward swing."

The head should be steady, not rigid to the point of creating tension. Work on the practice tee to maintain a steady head position. Keep the head behind the ball through impact when the momentum of the swing will bring it up and around to the finish position. (For the record, there are some excellent professionals who do not let the right shoulder bring the head up and around, namely, Annika Sorenstam, David Duval, and Jim Furyk. These players release everything through impact.) One of the most common drills used to check for a steady head is to have someone hold the grip of a club on your head while you make a swing. This drill will help you to become aware of what your head does during the swing. It will help you to stop any head movement that you may have. Once you can "feel" what your head does, then you can monitor it. At the end of this chapter, you will see how to monitor all of your body parts during the swing.

A steady head promotes centeredness over the ball as well as balance throughout the swing. With a steady head, one can get away with other poor moves in the swing. Think of a golfer with a pole through the spinal column and the golfer just turns or pivots around it. This is the concept of the steady head during the swing.

Steady Head

- Centered over the ball.
- Full shoulder turn.
- Upper torso coiled over the lower body.
- Right side fully "loaded."

Tilt
Step 1

Hold a club vertically from your chin down to the middle of your stance. The club shaft should bisect your sternum.

Tilt
Step 2

Then, tilt your body (and head) so that the handle of the club points to the instep of the front foot.

THE SHOULDERS. The shoulders are parallel to the line at address, with the left shoulder slightly higher than the right one due to the right hand being lower on the grip. The left shoulder turns to the right and tilts down a little more so that it will get under the chin at the top of the backswing. The right shoulder rises up and to the rear. At the top of the backswing the shoulders should be at least perpendicular to the line. That is, the left shoulder should turn at least 90 degrees to the right and point downward toward the ball while the head is steady. (There is an exception for the "X-factor" golfers, in that their shoulders stay more level in the backswing.) The more you can turn the shoulders the better. Supple golfers can achieve 100-plus degrees of shoulder turn. At the top of the backswing the left shoulder should be touching the chin. The back should be facing the target. If you can achieve this position, then you have made a full turn.

The average golfer usually has his head stooped over too much at address, which puts the chin into the chest. This means the chin gets in the way during the backswing. This can cause several problems, including an incomplete shoulder turn, some lift in the backswing, head movement, or even an upper body swaying instead of a coiling. All of these moves can result in a loss of power, mis-hits, and frustration.

Starting down, the shoulders lag behind the lower body. Avoid trying to speed up the right shoulder until the club head has reached the impact area. Then, turn on the speed. Let the right shoulder fire through the ball along with the right hip, knee and foot. This right side firing action provides additional power. At the top of the backswing, however, the transition into the through-swing must begin with a coordinated lower body movement.

At and during impact, the left shoulder is in an upward thrusting move and is slightly past being parallel to the target. The right shoulder is moving down and under the left shoulder, and is back behind the golfer's head. (It should feel as if the whole right shoulder area, the shoulder, upper arm, and lats, are turning into the ball with speed.) The left shoulder continues to move up and back as the right shoulder moves up and around. The shoulders catch up to the lower body at the finish of the swing. They should be level and face the target along with the rest of the body.

THE ARMS. At address the arms are relaxed, comfortable and hang freely from the shoulder sockets. They should not be reaching for the ball. The arms swing the club to the top of the backswing. The backswing is initiated by an almost simultaneous movement of the left arm, hand, shoulder, the latissimus dorsi, and the left hip all turning to the right. This movement is referred to as the "one-piece takeaway" and also includes the rolling of the instep of the left foot to the right, which in turn, pulls the left knee and leg towards the right leg in preparation for the right side "loading" on the backswing. Ben Hogan felt that the extension of the left arm and the turning of the shoulders pulled the left hip into its rotation on the backswing. Many current instructors teach that this movement happens almost simultaneously.

Even though you can monitor this action, it is something that the golfer shouldn't be thinking about. Just try to let it happen. If you want to monitor this feeling when you are on the practice tee, do the following. Stand away from the ball and close your eyes. Take a swing and concentrate on when your hips begin to move and how they move. "Feel" if they move together with the arms and hands and shoulders. Or, "feel" if they move a split second afterwards and are being pulled into their rotation. You can monitor the movement of all of your body parts in this way. I call this the "eyes shut monitoring system." It will be discussed in more detail, along with some examples, later in the book. You must know what to look for and what you should be able to feel. At the top of the swing, the arms and hands do nothing but wait their turn to deliver their stored up power. (All of the players who hit the ball a long way have remarkably "passive" hands.) The proficient golfers always start the downswing with the lower body move that drops the arms and hands and the club into the slot. The hands and arms are therefore, in essentially the same position as they were at the top. As the body rotation continues into and through the impact area, then the arms and hands can deliver their force. At this point in the swing, the greater the arm speed the farther you will hit the ball. Tiger Woods exemplifies the speed of the body rotation as well as arm and shoulder speed through the ball. Remember that all of this occurs with "passive" hands.

THE HIPS. As previously mentioned, Ben Hogan felt that the correct order of movement for the backswing is the hands, arms and shoulders (almost simultaneously) and that this movement pulled the hips into their proper turning motion. Consequently, the turning of the hips pulled the left leg in to the right. All of this occurred in a split-second unified action.

The backswing represents a torsion action (or tension) created between the shoulder turn and the hip turn that stores the energy of the upper torso in the backswing. It is this tension that allows the golfer to get the "pulling" action on the through-swing. There is also tension built up in the muscles of the inside of the thighs due to the hip turn. This stores up energy in the lower body. It is this tension that enables the golfer to "fire" the right side during impact and beyond. These two actions of "pulling" and "firing" are very powerful ones that were created because of the proper windup in the backswing. When this windup is properly achieved, the through-swing should occur on its own – just as in the example of the toy top.

The hips are one of the most important, if not the most significant, power generators that the golfer has. Therefore, proper use of the hips is the key to solid, consistent ball striking. What do the hips do in the swing? Earlier, we talked about the one-piece takeaway to the swing. That is, the near simultaneous movement of the left side (hands, arms and shoulders, and roll of the left foot) that cause the hips to begin their turning clockwise a split-second later. The one-piece movement with good extension should turn the hips the proper amount, at least 45 degrees. Some of the great players actually have more than a 45-degree turn. For example, Nicklaus and Norman turn their hips almost 60 degrees.

The hips do not stay level on the backswing; the left hip tilts downward about 20 degrees from the horizontal. If the hips stayed level on the backswing, the swing would get too flat and the club would get too far behind the golfer. When this happens, the results usually are weak, blocked shots to the right; or the result can be a quick turn-down hook due to the body being unable to get out of the way on the through-swing and the hands taking over too soon in the swing. The hip turn, or rotation, essentially coordinates the rest of the body movement on the backswing. Proper turning of the hips permits the golfer to get the maximum extension and the proper position at the top.

The right hip moves up and back. It does not move laterally. The right side and leg is essentially in the same position that it was at address. With the proper turning of the hips, the right side should "load" (store energy) and be in a position to "fire" the lower body at the proper time in the through-swing. It is almost universally agreed that the through-swing or (downswing) begins with the turning of the hips to the left, or, at the very least, a coordinated movement of the lower body. (There are few, if any, modern day golf instructors who would advocate starting down with an upper body move.) The coordinated lower body movement, in and of itself, allows all of the power stored up on the backswing to be released in the proper sequence in the through-swing.

Years ago, a well-known teacher invented the term "SLURN" when he referred to the first move back into the ball. SLURN is an acronym for the slide (lateral move) and turn of the hips to the left to begin the downswing. Though it is a catchy term, it can cause misunderstandings. For example, what is the right amount of lateral move? It is quite nebulous. If a golfer has a strong grip, he must make a greater lateral move than a golfer who has a weak grip. Why? Because if the golfer with a strong grip made a "normal" lateral move back into the ball, his club face would be closed at impact causing hooks or pulls. Therefore, he must move farther laterally to get the face square. Paul Azinger is a good example of a professional who has a strong grip and makes a larger than normal lateral move. Many low handicappers have an over-exaggerated lateral move of the hips from the top, which can cause inconsistencies. A player also needs very strong hands and wrists to be able to hold the proper angles during an over-exaggerated lateral move.

Remember that the hips turn in a clockwise manner during the backswing, and they tilt about 20 degrees from the horizontal. The through-swing should produce motion that is just the reverse of this, namely, a turning action on an upward angle. The shoulders, arms and hands, in that order, follow this movement. The very long hitters actually create additional tension or torsion between the hips and shoulders at the initiation of the through-swing. The hips must get out of the way of the upper torso so that the power in the upper torso can be fully released. The power stored in the lower body is released through the transfer of the weight from the right side to the left side and from the rotation of the body. Since the hips have been wound up tightly on the backswing, the faster they move once you are in the impact area, the more power will be generated.

"Pull"

- Starting down, the lower body's unified action starts the through-swing.

- The arms and club are dropping into the "slot".

- The left arm is "pulling" down.

"Fire"

- In the impact area, the right side is unloading or "firing" its stored energy through the ball.

- Note the "bracing" of the left leg. It is still in a flex condition, not rigid.

THE KNEES. At address, both knees should be pointed or tucked inward. However, be sure not to create any tension when you tuck them in. On the back-swing, the left knee should point slightly behind the ball while the right knee is maintained in the same relative position that it was at address. It will not stay in this same position. It will move slightly. But, it should never be placed into a "locked" position where it becomes straight and rigid. If it does, it will hinder the "firing" action of the right side. When the right knee is tucked in at address, that helps place it in the proper position to support the "loading" of the right foot, leg and hip joint at the top of the backswing. The knees (and legs) should have a feeling of being springy at address and throughout the swing. It is this springiness that allows you to obtain a good swinging action, deliver a powerful blow to the ball at impact, and swing to a full finish.

On the through-swing, the golfer should strive for the feeling that the right knee is driving at and through the ball. The left knee, at impact, has moved to the left of where it was at address and should be pointed about halfway between the original ball position and the target. Both knees should face the target at the finish of the swing.

THE LEGS. With proper foot action, the correct leg action will follow. The legs should feel springy at address. On the backswing, the "loading", (the effect of the weight transfer from the left side), should be felt on the inside of the thigh and calf of the right leg. Do not let the right leg to become rigid. Maintain the springiness in it that you had at address. Meanwhile, at the top, the left leg has developed some muscle tension along the inside of it. Keep in mind that the muscles used in the legs are on the inside of each leg. On the through-swing, the golfer should feel as if he is "unloading" the inside of the right thigh and calf (as well as the right knee) at and through the ball. The left leg is braced for the thrusting of the right side. The left leg remains flexed, not straight, for the bracing action and the weight is maintained along the inside of it during impact. At the finish, the left leg supports the weight almost entirely.

THE FEET. At address, the golfer should be able to wiggle his toes inside of his shoes to help stay relaxed. Also, the weight should be distributed equally on the inside (or balls) of the feet. Some accomplished players set a little more weight on the right foot at address so they can get behind the ball easier. But, if the player uses a forward press to start the backswing, then he should start with the weight equally on both feet.

On the backswing, the left foot rolls to the left on the inside of the ball of the foot. It is okay to let the left heel raise slightly off of the ground, although most modern professionals keep their left foot on the ground. To raise or not to raise the left heel depends largely on the individual's flexibility. This transfer of weight is shifted to the inside of the right foot and is known as "loading" the right foot. Some players feel that this "loading" takes place on the heel as well as the inside of the ball of the right foot.

On the through-swing, the transfer of weight is reversed. The left foot rolls back to the right to prepare for the bracing action during impact. The weight is transferred to the inside of the ball of the left foot. The foot continues to roll until the weight is on the outside of the foot at the finish of the swing. The right foot rolls to the left and "kicks off" during impact. (Some modern day instructors have their students try to feel as if they keep the right foot on the ground during impact. Usually, this is for individuals who have an overly active leg drive during the through-swing.) You should get use to "kicking off" and thrusting the right side into and through the ball.

The momentum of the body rotation and the swinging of the club cause the right foot to end up on the right toe with very little weight on it at the finish. A very good practice drill is to "walk through" the shot just as Gary Player does. At the finish, if you are in balance, you should be able to take a step forward toward your target and simply start walking. This drill promotes a properly balanced and rhythmic swing that is necessary to strike the ball consistently well.

George Knudsen, who played on the PGA tour and was an excellent ball striker, believed that his feet totally controlled his swing. He used to feel as if he was rocking back and forth on the insides of his feet to give him a "loading" and "unloading" action. So, roll on the inside of the left instep. "Load" on the inside of the right foot. Then, "fire" or "unload" the inside of the right foot; and, "brace" or "load" the inside of the left foot. Let the weight finish almost entirely on the left foot.

THE TRIANGLE: The arms hang freely from the shoulders at address. The elbows should point approximately toward the hips. The arms, hands and shoulders form a triangle. This triangle should be maintained during the swing. Some teachers have their students extend the triangle back as their first move on the backswing. By taking the triangle back in this way, it is a one-piece takeaway.

The following story will help amplify this concept. About 32 years ago, I met a well-known and highly respected teaching professional named Harry Pressler. Harry was a wonderful person. Harry worked with a number of women professional golfers who played the LPGA tour; the most famous of whom was Mickey Wright. Harry used to come to Montecito Country Club during the summer months, as those were the hot months in the Palm Springs area where he gave golf lessons during the rest of the year. Montecito used to have a small practice area above the clubhouse parking lot, across from the 16th tee. His teaching methods were not complex. He did have a few training devices. One of them was simply an elastic band about six inches wide and 14 to 18 inches long. He had the ends sewn together so that it became a circular band. He would have the golfer wrap it around her arms so that it was in place slightly above the elbows. Then, once this triangle was formed, he would have her hit shots with the wrap on. This proved to be an excellent drill. (One can do this with a bungy cord as well.)

Harry would teach the ladies the "over and under" swing method. Simply put, on the backswing, the club is swung with the arms "over" the breast area; and on the through-swing the club is swung with the arms "under" the breast area. A very simple drill, yet it helps a golfer not have to think about swing plane or other complexities of the swing (assuming the golfer had the proper stance, alignment, and posture). When you think about it, the club is always coming into the line from the inside path. Assuming the golfer has the correct rotation or pivoting on the through-swing, the club then travels down the line and back to the inside. It is simple, easy and correct.

On the backswing, the triangle should be extended comfortably as far as it can be until the hands are hip high. Then the arms continue to swing the club upwards to the top. This is a motion coordinated with the body turn on the backswing. It is not a "lifting" motion of the arms. The arms should stay relaxed. The forearms rotate clockwise on the backswing and counterclockwise on the through-swing. This forearm rotation should not be a conscious effort. It should occur on its own. If it doesn't, you will "broom" the ball. That is, there will be no release of the club through the ball, and you will have weak, ugly shots.

Training Aid

See how nicely the triangle is formed using the elastic wrap training aid.

Training Aid

"Over" using the training aid.

Training Aid

"Under" using the training aid.

On the through-swing, the arms (and hands) are the last power generator in the sequencing of the swing. Once the initial move has dropped the arms and hands into the "slot", the faster the arm speed the better. (As a matter of fact, many instructors now teach that if you just swing the arms, the body rotation will take care of itself.) The following drill is a good way to feel how the arms work during the swing. Stand with your feet close together and just swing the arms back to the top and through to a finish. Stay in balance while you are doing this drill. If you have a weighted club or hold three of your irons together and do this drill, you can build up a swinging motion, gain arm speed and flexibility, and add some strength to your arms.

The left arm should feel as if it is "pulling" down and through the ball. It should be straight at impact. The right arm is not straight at impact; it straightens out a little bit after impact and just before your arms reach hip high on the follow-through. The left arm folds immediately after the full arm extension on the follow-through and the right arm is fully extended at the finish. The finish is almost a mirror image of the position at the top of the backswing.

Arm Swing Drill

With your feet close together, hit short irons to feel how the arm swing works

THE HANDS. Active hands can ruin a golf swing. Some of the problems attributed to having active hands include:

- Causing a golfer to take the club away with a jerky first move.

- Creating "lift" in the swing causing a false turn on the backswing.

- Causing a golfer to "cast" the club from the top.

- Causing a golfer to either release too early on the through-swing (resulting in a hook); or release too late on the through-swing (resulting in a blocked shot or a slice).

The hands should be passive during the swing until they get to the impact area where they can pour on their power. If the bigger muscles of the body start the club back in a one-piece motion, and the arms are extended fully, and the shoulders and hips make their full turn to the top, then the hands have worked as they should. They have held on to the club and were passive all the way to the top. When the lower body move initiates the through-swing, the hands should feel as if they remained at the top. This is the passivity of the hands that good players strive for because it tells them that the bigger muscles of the body are working properly to supply their power. The hands and arms have not overridden them. At impact, both of the hands, release their energy through the uncocking of the wrists. There can be no loosening of the club during this time. This is the principle reason for having the right grip pressure, i.e., the club is traveling very fast by this time in the swing and there is a vibration felt in the hands due to the club coming into contact with the ball.

THE WRISTS. The wrists are simply used as a hinge. They hinge on the backswing and unhinge on the through-swing during impact. Some accomplished players set their wrists earlier than others during the backswing. It is recommended that average golfers and beginners make no conscious effort to hinge their wrists. Because the club is being swung to the top, it creates momentum. This momentum will cause a hinging of the wrists. This hinging or cocking of the wrists is also known as "setting" the club at the top. As a general rule, the deeper the "set", the farther you will hit the ball. The deep "set" can only be accomplished with the correct grip, which keeps the club under control at the top. Practice this drill for setting the club. Hold the club with your arms extended straight out in front of you so that the club shaft is horizontal to the ground. Then cock your wrists. The club shaft should now be vertical to the ground. Then turn your shoulders clockwise to the top of the backswing. This is your "set" position. Do not try for any other "set" position.

Setting the Club Drill
Step 1

Hold the club in front of you as shown.

Setting the Club Drill
Step 2

Raise the club to a vertical position by cocking your wrists.

Setting the Club Drill
Step 3

Make a full shoulder turn to the top of the backswing while keeping the set position of step 2.

THE EYES SHUT MONITORING SYSTEM

The prior section described how the body parts work and what you should be able to feel during the swing. It was necessary to go into these descriptions so that you can troubleshoot your swing. It is simple and easy to do. You can monitor any part of your swing by using the eyes shut monitoring system, ESMS. How does ESMS work? Close your eyes and make a swing without swinging at a ball. Keep the club about 8 to 12 inches above the ground at take a practice swing. Feel the freedom in the swing. When swinging, focus on a particular body part. Monitor how it moves. Determine if it is moving in the same way as described in the previous section. The following examples will illustrate how you can use ESMS.

With your eyes closed, make a practice swing and focus on the rolling of the left foot on its instep. Feel the weight begin to shift to the right. Then do it again. Focus on how the left knee begins to break behind the ball. Feel if you are lifting your left heel too much or not at all when the left knee breaks inward. Is the weight on the instep of the left foot during impact? Do you feel properly braced? Are you finishing in balance?

Take another swing with your eyes closed. Feel what your right foot is doing. Is it "loading" the transfer of weight to the inside of the right instep? Is the weight moving to the outside of the right foot? Take another swing with your eyes closed. Monitor the action of your hips. Is your left hip turning or swaying on the backswing? Is it tilting slightly downward? Is the right hip moving back and slightly up? Can you feel the weight being transferred to the inside joint of the right hip? Continue swinging with your eyes closed, and each time focus on a different part of your swing. Are your shoulders turning fully? Are they perpendicular to the line at the top of the backswing? In another swing, see if the right shoulder is moving down and under during impact? And, yet again in another swing, see if you are getting a left-side elongation during impact? Is the left shoulder moving up and back? You get the idea. Try this when you go to the practice range, and do it on the golf course after you make a poor shot. It just may tell you what is going wrong.

In this context, let me tell you a story of what happened to me recently. I hadn't played for about a week, principally due to the writing of the section on the workings of the body parts. Prior to the round, I went to the range to loosen up and get some rhythm into my swing. It all started out okay. Then my guest arrived and we started to talk about some of his swing problems. A little later a friend of mine was just leaving the course and he stopped by to chat. After he left, I went back to hitting balls. It was awful. My pace was fast. I didn't have any control of the shots. The driver was pitiful. I remarked to my playing partners that it could be a long day if I didn't settle down.

On the way to the tee, I was thinking about how to slow my mind and swing. I bogeyed the first hole, but hit a crisp 7-iron on the par-three second. This tuned me into what I had just done. I closed my eyes and went to the side of the tee and made a practice swing after my playing partners had hit their shots. The light went on. My lower body was moving too fast too soon. It was way out of sync with the rest of my swing. From that point on, I slowed my hip move down and hit the ball solidly for the rest of the round. The eyes shut monitoring system works!

ESMS.

At the top, monitoring "width."

ESMS — Starting Down

Monitoring hips and lower body.

ESMS — Impact

Monitoring the "brace" of the left leg.

Chapter 4
THE MENTAL SIDE OF THE GAME

Believe in yourself. Learn who you are — what you are — and your limitations. Then work and play within these limitations. Be true to yourself. For example, suppose that you were faced with a shot that required a carry of 230 yards to get to the fairway. And your best drive ever was 230 yards, including roll. Obviously, you would look for a safer line on which to hit the ball. Use good judgment. Look for the highest percentage play. Manage your golf ball, within your capabilities. Always play to your strengths. Try to make the next shot easier.

In order to play well, you must have both tactics and a strategy. The strategy is the plan of attack for the golf course, and the tactics are the ways in which you implement that strategy or game plan. In this chapter, we are going to discuss the mental preparation required for a successful game plan.

Earlier, we described the principles of **F-A-C-E**, which stands for:

Focus And Commit to and Execute the shot at hand. The Focus and Commit stages are mental processes that result in the third stage, Execute, the mechanical process.

Focus: As you prepare to make your shot, there must be total concentration, weighing every aspect of the shot, including weather conditions, the position of the pin, the lie of the ball, the shape of the shot to get it to the landing area, the highest percentage type of shot to get it there, and the club selection. All decisions made at this stage must be made with conviction. There can be no doubt. If you are uncertain about any aspect, reconsider it until you are completely sure about it. Once you are certain, visualize the shape of the shot; whether it is to be a low punch shot, or a high, soft draw, for example. Do not second-guess yourself during the shot. Jack Nicklaus always talked about his visualization process being a three-step process. He would see where he wanted the ball to come to rest, shape the shot in his mind to get it there, and use the set up and swing to play it the way he thought it out.

Commit: Being absolutely certain about your decision in the focusing stage means that you can commit to the shot with full confidence. It also helps you to relax during the swing because of the certainty that you had in the focusing stage; you know that you are playing the right shot for the situation. If you aren't sure if a shot calls for a 6-iron or a 7-iron, then confusion sets in. The mind is puzzled.

You become tentative. And, maybe even tense. Under these circumstances, you have very little chance of hitting a good shot. Being certain in the focusing stage allows you to commit completely to your shot. Remember to:

- Go all out.

- Don't hold back.

- Commit fully and execute.

Tiger Woods has a complete grasp of these mental processes and therefore does not hold back once his mind is made up. He has great confidence in his ability to play the proper shot. And, he trusts his skills to execute it.

Execute: The execution of a shot is a result of the focus and commitment. The time and concentration spent on focusing will allow you to commit with full confidence. Good thought processes allow the golfer to swing the club (or putt) with greater confidence while being more relaxed. He therefore increases the probability of hitting the shot as planned. Of course, this assumes that his mental planning was within his abilities to pull off the shot as planned. *Execution of the shot is the final piece of a perfect thought-mechanical procedure,* **F-A-C-E.**

When you are in the zone, it is as if the mind is taking a long, quiet nap. The mind doesn't get in the way. It is uncluttered and at peace. The confidence level is at its peak. You know that you can make any shot or hole any putt. Your awareness is heightened. The action occurring in the round is what it is all about. You are just letting it happen. The mind is quiet and on autopilot. And, so is the body. There are little, if any, beta brain waves (analytical thinking). There are basically only alpha brain waves (thinking stops). In other words, if you think too much you can get "paralysis by analysis." This is precisely what you do not want because it can take you out of the zone. You may even find yourself humming a tune, or a melody may be playing inside your mind that is soothing and refreshing, having the effect of quieting your nerves. There is no distraction, no tension, and no muscle contraction. They simply cannot penetrate the quietness of the mind.

In this context, let me tell you a story. Recently, I shot my age, 68. It was one of my goals for the year. It was so easy, but I was aided with my 12th hole-in-one. I had a birdie and a bogey and 15 pars. My index varies between 4.5 and 5.5. Our course is a par 70 and is rated 71.2. The slope is 126. What I felt during that round were all of the "in the zone" feelings I just listed. I was having fun. My mind was very quiet. And, I couldn't get a hymn out of my mind. It was the Sanctus Acclamation, which concludes the introduction to the Eucharistic Prayer at Mass. I couldn't get the "Hosanna in the Highest" part out of my head. It kept going round and round in my mind for days.

Having a quiet, uncluttered mind is the ultimate requisite for playing in the zone. It allows one to concentrate and relax. The question then arises: Can this state of mind be achieved on a regular, even daily basis? I don't know. But, I do know that the truly great players of my era, such as Hogan, Snead, Nelson, Palmer and Nicklaus, seem to have achieved it more regularly than other players of that era. Hogan and Palmer always reached for that perfect synergy of concentration and relaxation. The principles of **F-A-C-E** provide the basis for the perfect thought-mechanical procedure. Through practice, these principles can be learned. Once learned, they can and should become a regular part of your pre-shot routine. And, isn't that what concentration (the mental preparation for the shot) and relaxation (the body and mind must not be tense or cluttered respectively, for the mechanical execution of the shot) really means?

Currently, Tiger Woods seems to play in the zone quite regularly. Tiger knows what he can and can't do. He maps out a strategy for a golf course, believes in it and implements it. He prepares by being well conditioned mentally and physically. His skill level is exceptional, as is his ability to execute the fundamentals of the game. He is quick to understand any weakness he may have with respect to the course he is preparing for. And he promptly corrects it through hard work in the practice area. He has great discipline and self-control and appears to be at his best when his best is needed. He knows that there are no short cuts to achieving his best. He shows a love for the game, its history and the competition of the battle. What is truly amazing is that he always seems confident and prepared. Having confidence is to know that you are prepared.

Tim Gallwey, the author of *Inner Golf,* developed some mental drills that can help golfers improve their concentration skills. His drills are based upon learned behavior. He argues that learning is directly proportional to the quality of concentration. The drills help the golfer obtain a quiet state of mind, the feeling of "letting go". It is good reading and the drills on this subject can help.

When reflecting on the past year and one-half on the PGA tour, it seems that when Davis Love III has been paired with Tiger Woods, Davis appeared to be unable to reach a state of mind necessary to outduel Tiger. It is supposition on my part, but it brings some questions to mind. Namely, did Davis have his mental attitude sufficiently developed to win? Or, was it that Tiger played better in each case? Perhaps Davis really did reach down to his inner depth, as deep as he could, and it wasn't enough to win.

I ask these questions not to denigrate Davis, because the questions could apply to many golfers in many situations, but to encourage you to look at your own game. Are you getting the most out of your talent? Are you being the best that you can be? Who can ask any more than you give it all that you can? If you can do this, that is all that is expected. If you have given it your all and it isn't good enough to win, then that is the way it is supposed to be.

If your round is not happening positively for you on the course, don't try to make things happen. On the contrary, relax and try to get your mind to have freer flowing thoughts and allow your swing to flow more freely and easily. Think of it as mind tension and physical tension. Relax and enjoy the game. Try to determine what is interfering or has interfered with your positive thoughts. Then, just let it happen.

I used to play with an assistant professional who was a very good player but never reached his potential due to an uncontrollable temper. One time in a tournament, he had hit several poor wedge shots and missed a few short putts during the round but he was able to control himself during the course of play. However, an hour or so after the round was finished, his rage got to him. While he was driving home from the tournament on a four-lane road, he stopped his car on the shoulder between the fast lane and the barrier for oncoming traffic, and opened the trunk. He proceeded to pull a wedge out of the golf bag and break it over the barrier fence. He then took his putter, tied it to the bumper of his car with a piece of rope, and let it drag on the road all the way home. This is meant to be funny, and in one sense it is, however, it illustrates a complete lack of discipline and self-control, not to mention a person who was obviously not enjoying the game. He no longer plays the game of golf. The moral is: This kind of mindset can and will hurt a player, either during the round or after it. Don't throw clubs. Don't pound your clubs on the ground. Do not talk negatively to yourself after a mis-hit or a mental error. If you start out poorly in a round, or have a bad hole during the round, keep telling yourself that you will play well from that point on. Set new goals during the round. You are always better off thinking about the really good shots you hit or the solid putts you stroked. This gives you positive feedback, which is essential to helping you to play your best. Champions like Davis Love III try to play every shot to the best of their ability.

Playing in the zone always keeps you thinking positively and eliminates fear and anxiety, which are major contributors to mis-hits. If you get it to two under par, think three under, and if you get it to three under, think four under and so on. If you have your opponent down by three with nine holes to play, think about closing him out at seven and five. Never think that you just want to hold on to the lead. It is a recipe for disaster. As golfers will tell you, when you are in the zone, you don't get in your own way. Recently, Notah Begay, in an interview after shooting a 59, said: "You can do anything on those days. You can't do anything wrong. Even the bounces go your way."

In early December 1999, the Discovery Channel aired a program on science and the mind. In one segment, they showed a marksman as he was sighting-in a target (a bulls-eye). The marksman was wired to a monitor to record his alpha and beta brain waves. The gun had a laser beam attached to it. While sighting-in on the bullseye, his beta brain waves were very active. The laser beam was all over the place and not on the bulls-eye, indicating that he was thinking too much. But, once he sighted-in on the bullseye and had the laser beam focused, the beta waves stopped and the alpha waves started. These alpha waves were much calmer than the beta waves indicating that he was ready to commit with confidence. Then, BANG! Bullseye!

Why is this example interesting? How does it relate to golf or other sports? Let's break it down:

The high activity of the brain waves occurs during the Focus And Commit stages of the process. Whether it is zeroing in on a bullseye or preparing to play a high fade over a pond of water to a green, each individual must go through a mental process. Remember that the brain is the control center for virtually all of our vital activities. It also controls sleep, hunger, thirst, and emotions. The brain receives and interprets countless signals that are sent to it from other parts of the body and from the external environment. The brain controls our motor functions and muscle movement. It coordinates all motor activity from hitting a golf ball to pulling the trigger of a gun. The high brain wave activity of the marksman illustrates just what is described here. He is receiving information, assembling/decoding it, and preparing to transmit. That is to say, once his brain is satisfied with this processing effort (the Focus stage), he will be ready (Commit stage) to fire his gun at the bulls-eye with a high confidence level that he will hit the target. The beta waves indicate that the marksman is thinking and analyzing.

With respect to the calm brain wave pattern, I believe that the marksman became fully satisfied with his Focus and Commitment processes and he "knew" that he would hit the bullseye. He had quit thinking and was confident and relaxed. The laser beam focus on the bullseye had provided him the necessary feedback to commit fully with confidence to the Execution of the shot (pulling the trigger of the gun.) In this context, how many times have you believed that you were going to make a putt in advance of stroking it; or hit a shot just as you had planned it? Your concentration was total and you were calm and relaxed. This can be described as the perfect thought-mechanical procedure, namely, Focus And Commit and Execute, F-A-C-E.

The average golfer has a hard time concentrating well enough to arrive at the calm (alpha) wave state. He is usually trying to play a shot while still in the beta brain wave state. This is known as "paralysis by analysis." Watch the professional golfers go through their pre-shot routine. Each one has developed a routine that fits in with his or her individual personality. When their game is on, they are achieving the alpha state more often than not. The more one can achieve this state of mind, the higher the level of golf one can play. I believe that this is what golfers mean when they say that they have taken their game to another level. Their confidence level soars. They are getting good feedback about their shotmaking. For example, when a golfer visualizes a particular type of shot, and after striking the ball, he looks up and sees it starting on line to the target; it is this kind of feedback that every golfer looks for. When a golfer can do this two or three times in a row during a round or on the practice tee, his confidence soars. This is a key factor in gaining confidence because you are integrating the mental and mechanical processes and getting good feedback. Professional golfers strive for this feedback.

Often a golfer will start his round feeling great, with high expectations of shooting a low score, or having a career round. The golfer feels like the opponent doesn't have a chance in the match. Before the round, he was striking the ball well on the range. He had performed his pre-game stretching exercises. On the practice putting green his "touch" was good. This is his day! However, after a solid drive, he comes off his approach shot a little and plugs the ball under the lip of the right bunker guarding the first green. He can't get the ball out toward the target. He must play it backwards into the middle of the bunker. Double bogey. What a start.

The round continues to degenerate. No matter how hard he tries, he just can't seem to muster anything positive out of his round. Even the bounces are not going his way. He is really trying but his muscles are a little tighter than normal. His legs are not springy, in fact, they are tired. He can't quite get that relaxed feeling.

Such a round happened to me recently. Ever since I shot my age, I have expectations of doing it again every time I tee it up. This day was a beautiful day for playing golf, but it was a disastrous day for me in terms of meeting my expectations. From the outset of the round, I struggled with my game. I am sure that my playing companions thought that I was in a brooding state of mind. And, perhaps I was. But I always try to think positive. I do not indulge in negative self-talk because that kind of mindset doesn't do any good. The bounces were not going my way, nor were the putts. I was hitting good putts and they were not going into the hole. I had five or six lip-outs. It seemed that everything that I did was inadequate that day. The hole seemed as if there was cellophane over it. The only thing that saved it for me were the two glorious shots on the finishing hole. The hole is a demanding 440-yard, dogleg right, par 4. It has a stream on the right side starting at about 200 yards from the tee and it runs all the way up the right side to the green. After a solid drive into the center of the fairway, I had 165 yards to the front of the green. The pin was on the right side of the green and was 25 yards deep. The green is uphill on the approach shot and has two bunkers on the right side between the green and the stream; and it has two bunkers on the left side. The approach shot was slightly downwind and I decided to play a 5-iron and hit a high fade into the green. The shot came off as I had visualized it and ended up hole high about 18 feet left of the hole.

Those two shots, the drive and the 5-iron approach shot, were the only two shots that came off as planned that day; the principles of **F-A-C-E** were carried out. It turned an otherwise frustrating day, both mentally and physically, into a positive day. That is precisely what every golfer has to take away from these types of rounds. I never doubted my capability to perform. It was simply that I was more tired than I had imagined. My mind was wandering. My concentration was poor. My body, even though it felt good on the range, was tired. I simply couldn't get out of my own way that day. The amazing thing was that I was able to implement a sound thought-mechanical process on that last hole. For some reason, my mental pre-shot routine was such that I knew I was going to hit good shots. My focus was intense without being tense. My concentration level was heightened. Hitting those two shots was a very positive thing that I took away from the round. It made my day.

Why does this kind of round happen? I don't know. But, I have had those rounds, and I am sure that everyone else who has ever played golf has had them as well. Maybe it happens because your body chemistry is upset, too much or too little adrenaline. Or, perhaps you have too much tension that day. Maybe you can't get business matters out of your mind. The list can go on and on. In any event, any number of these occurrences can be reasons for these "bad" days. It could also be due to being over-confident at the outset and not realizing that the mind and body are tired. In this state, it is difficult to concentrate and apply the principles of **F-A-C-E**. Despite all that has been said about applying these principles, there will be occasional days where nothing seems to work. Professionals have these days too, however, they recognize them more quickly than amateurs do. I have talked with a number of professionals about this problem, and when asked what they do on those days, they all say the same thing – try to get into the clubhouse with a score that keeps you in the event; don't post a big number; don't take yourself out of the event.

When you encounter one of these frustrating days, and recognize it, try and do the following after the round. Reflect back on the circumstances surrounding the situation. Try to understand what happened. Were you tense? Did you let your mind wander? Were you thinking too much about swing mechanics or the errands you had to run after the round? Obviously, that "peace of mind" state was missing. What can be done about it? You can go to the range and beat balls to relieve frustration and tension. But this may not solve the basic cause of the problem. If you feel it is a swing fault, get with a professional for help. If it is due to mind clutter, then really work hard on the principles of **F-A-C-E**. Imagine that you are playing different holes in your practice sessions. Shape your shots. Hit a high fade, then a low draw, a punch shot, and so on. Visualize the shape of the shot. **F**ocus on how you are going to get the ball to the target. Make a full and total **C**ommitment to it. Then, let the **E**xecution just happen. The mental processes of focusing and committing to the shot allow the mechanical process of executing it to happen with a higher probability of success. One fun way to relax on the practice range is to start using different clubs to hit a specific target. For example, let's say that you normally fly a five iron 170 yards. Pick a target, about 120 yards away and hit the 5-iron to it. Do the same thing for a variety of targets using different irons. Try it and you may begin to enjoy the game more. These practice range exercises will at least help relieve tension.

Trust what you are doing. When you do, this learning (and trusting) process can be taken from the practice range to the golf course. That is the rationale for applying the principles of **F-A-C-E**. The more golfers can apply these principles, the closer they get to entering the zone.

Applying these principles and frequently using the "eyes shut monitoring system" are stepping stones towards this passageway. These are simple ways to condition your mind. They will influence your swing, both on the course and the range, in a positive way. Golfers who think like champions implement these processes more often than not. They have conditioned their minds for the competition and the heat of the battle. They are positive that they can get the ball from point A to point B as planned. They trust their swing and let their mind do the work.

It was stated earlier that 90% of this game is played between the ears. It involves discipline, character and the power of positive thinking. It is you pitting everything, every ounce of know-how that you can muster, against the golf course. It is the ultimate struggle of one against oneself. As Tom Watson so aptly put it during the famous shootout with Jack Nicklaus at the 1977 British Open in Turnberry, Scotland: "This is what it is all about, isn't it?" To which Nicklaus replied, "Yes." Both of those golfers are true champions. And, that was a great contest. In that shootout, both men excelled. There was no fear or apprehension. Their minds were in full control. They were, essentially, feeding off of one another's play. They both knew that they could play whatever shot they needed to play, and for two days, they did. Both men were in the zone. Watson shot 131; and Nicklaus shot 132! It was exciting to watch.

Obstacles do not exist in the zone. It is as if you could play the shots blind-folded. Like you have the laser beam focus of the marksman. There seems to be no difficulty out there. It is like the old Johnny Mercer lyrics "accentuate the positive, eliminate the negative, latch-on to the affirmative, and don't mess with mister in-between." The mind is calm. The muscles are under control and relaxed. The long, hard hours of practice are paying off. Your whole mind is devoted to playing the pre-determined shot in your pre-shot routine.

To quote an old Scottish axiom: "Golf is a game in which attitude of mind counts for incomparably more than the mightiness of muscle. Golf is a test of man's and woman's innermost self; of the soul and spirit, of character and disposition, of temperament and habit of mind." In other words, the contest is with oneself and the mastery of oneself. To that, however, we must include the golf course, with all of its elements to test our mental and physical capabilities. The purists would say that to play the game well the golfer must learn to keep his mind and body under control. Looking into oneself can enhance your potential to play well, but there is no guarantee that you will play well because of that.

Golf requires all of the fibers in the muscles of the hands, arms, feet, legs, hips, back and shoulders to be stimulated to action. To get all of these parts of the body synchronized to make a smooth, rhythmic swing so that you can make solid contact with the ball is a complex task. It requires enough practice to develop muscle and brain memory so that the swing can become repetitive. Neurologists refer to the education of sets of nerve cells and the fibers through which they function as associative memory. In his book on the five fundamentals of golf, Ben Hogan kept referring to muscle memory through practice as the basis for a sound golf swing. This is part but not all of it. The brain, using information principally from sight and touch, is the controlling force in telling the muscles what to do. The brain remembers good shots and bad ones and what was right or wrong. The sound of a golf ball being struck also provides feedback to the golfer. Hogan, along with many other great players, taught himself to remember the right things from this feedback information. So it is the brain, and how disciplined it is during the pre-shot routine, or how well it applies the principles of **F-A-C-E**, that is the basis for good shotmaking. I believe this is what Hogan referred to as concentration and relaxation, and why he was such a great golfer. He was the master of every golf shot.

The mental aspects of the game are the driving forces for the mechanical aspect. This is why the golfer needs to develop a sound thought-mechanical procedure, which, in and of itself, increases the probability of successful execution of the shot to be played. The probability of success takes into account a golfer's physical capability to perform the shot based on the mental preparation that preceded it.

For example, a golfer who has never hit a three-wood 200 yards on the fly wouldn't be planning a shot that had to carry that distance over a pond to the green. The golfer would look for alternative ways to play the hole and hopefully get his par. Remember that the perfect thought-mechanical procedure for every shot, whether a drive or a putt, is the key to playing the game better. The process should always include good judgment in deciding what is within the golfer's ability. In other words, you can precisely plan a shot but the execution of the shot may fail because your physical ability doesn't measure up to your mental capacity to visualize it.

It is important to not let a bad shot or a bad break upset you. Focus on the moment and stay in the present. Plan your recovery shot so that you can minimize the chances of putting a high number on the scorecard. Always play one shot at a time. Forget the previous one if it was not up to your standards.

There is another point that needs to be addressed here because it relates to being upset or possibly becoming upset. Occasionally, you may be paired with a person with whom you don't get along. These are the times that you must show respect for the game and your playing partners or your team (if you play on a high school or college team). Play the golf course. Be polite. Do not indulge in a lot of chatter. Concentrate on each drive, iron shot, approach shot and putt. Recognize that this pairing will test you and take it in stride. Do not allow yourself to get frustrated. Clear the mental mechanism, tune out the others and tune into yourself. Play a game with yourself. Perhaps you can play a game within a game. Keep a separate scorecard/journal on fairways hit, times in the first cut of rough, times in the primary rough, greens hit in regulation, number of one-putts, up and downs from bunkers or around the green, and so on. This game within a game exercise will help get your mind in order, and refocused on the game with yourself. You will be surprised at the results. After the round, reflect on the good things that happened and put them into your memory bank for future reference when other "adverse" pairings or situations occur. Always try to take something positive out of a round of golf, even if you did not play up to your expectations.

Let's summarize some of the key points on the mental aspects of the game. To begin with, the mind must be in command at all times for every shot, whether it is a drive, a long iron, a chip or a putt. The golfer must have a clear mental image of the shot to be played as well as the set up for how to play the shot. (Periodically, the golfer should use the eyes shut monitoring system to check on the set up image.)

Have a positive belief in yourself. Be positive at all times on every shot, and on every hole. Do not allow negative thoughts to enter your thought process as they can create tension that causes the muscles to tighten, thereby inhibiting a free flowing swing. Implementing the principles of **F-A-C-E** is essential for the highest probability of successfully executing each shot. In the event that your shot didn't come off as planned, prepare for the next shot in the same diligent manner. Trust and believe in yourself.

Keep your mind clear. Leave your business worries, family problems, and other external influences at home. These matters can and will affect the way you play. On those days when you are out on the course and things aren't going particularly well, try to relax and enjoy the company or the scenery. Do not let your score that day bother you. Try to take something positive out of the day.

Shooting my age was something special for me. I don't expect to shoot it everyday, even though deep down, I wish that I could. But I realize that it was out of the ordinary for me, given my capability. However, I set it as a goal again for this year. If I shoot my age again, fine and dandy, but if I don't, at least I know that I have continued to try very hard to accomplish it again. Setting goals is a positive thing that golfers at all levels should do.

High expectations often do not pan out. Let's say that you played a fine round of golf your last time out. You broke 80 for the first time. Now, you are thinking about shooting a 75 the next time. Your emotions are high. You go to the first tee all pumped up. You make a bad swing and drive the ball into a deep fairway bunker. This is a critical juncture in the round because it can set the tone for the rest of the day. This is the time when you must keep your emotions under control. Focus on the moment and the recovery shot. Stay in the present. Try to make the best score that you can on the hole, given the options available to you. Once the hole is completed, plan your strategy for the next hole. The following tip is for those days when you are aware of having high expectations. During your warm-up on the practice range, simulate playing the first two holes of the course. This will help to get you into a relaxed frame of mind and can help you get off to a good start. Golf is a game of skill, fun and enjoyment. It is also a very humbling game. It pits you (your body, mind and spirit) against the course and all of its elements. Success or failure is up to you. Accept the ups and downs of the game and think like a champion, whether or not you can play like one.

The Scots invented the game. They believed that God gave it to them as a penance and gave them scotch whiskey to ease their remorse. Remember that it is a game and should be played as a game. It should be played for the love of the game. That is the only way to play it.

A sound golf swing coupled with a positive mental attitude can help you love and enjoy playing the game to the best of your capabilities. Being "in the zone" is the ultimate pleasure of the game. It is an exalted state. Everything goes your way, including the bounces. Your mind is tranquil. The shots are easy to execute. The putts are going into the hole – center cut. Your score is low. What could be better? By applying the principles of **F-A-C-E**, you can find the zone more often than you are now.

There is a phrase that captures the essence of the negative aspects of the game. The phrase is "downward spiral." It happens in every sport. For example, baseball players have prolonged hitting slumps brought on by some mechanical flaw in their swing. During a batting slump, the player can lose confidence, which can cause a lack of concentration. The same is true in golf. The "downward spiral" can consist of many problems, including a lack of confidence and concentration, a build up of muscular and mental tension, and an inability to think properly. The harder a golfer tries, the worse it seems to get, adding poor results to the many bad bounces and bad breaks. It seems that the "law of averages" is unbalanced. Even "burn out" can occur. If this happens to you, take a few days off. Get away from the game. When you return your mind should be refreshed. Go back to the basics of the game, i.e., grip, stance, posture, and so on. Use the eyes shut monitoring system to check out the mechanical aspects of your swing. If you detect a swing flaw, correct it. Then work very hard on the mental side of the game, beginning at the practice area.

A golfer can stop the "downward spiral" by seriously adhering to the principles of **F-A-C-E**. Implement them at the practice range until you begin to see results and then take those results to the golf course. Focus intensely on each shot. Commit to each shot. Have confidence that you can make the shot. Act without thought of failure. Try to let it happen instinctively. Let the alpha waves happen. Be yourself, don't try to be someone else. Do not think swing mechanics. Trust your swing.

When you are ready to take this confidence to the golf course, play one shot at a time. Play to your strengths. Make a conscious effort to maintain good habits. Monitor your state of mind. Is your mind at peace? Are you able to execute the fundamentals of the game? Rate your ability to make good decisions. Are you keeping it simple and playing high percentage shots? Are you at ease on the course, or are you fighting yourself? Is your play commensurate with the amount of work that you are putting into the game? Have you set some short- and long-term goals for yourself? Are your emotions under control? Is your judgment satisfactory? Do you still have the desire to be better?

The three steps in the focusing process previously mentioned, were to first have a clear picture of where you want the ball to end up. Secondly, determine how you are going to shape the shot to get it there, and thirdly make sure that your set up is proper for the shape of the shot you are going to play. This process is the Focus stage. Once this imagery is clear to you, then you must commit to it with full confidence, (Commit stage.) You literally "see" the shot in your mind. This is referred to as conceptual imagery. There are many accomplished players, however, who use a different type of imagery or mental process, which I refer to as analytical imagery. It varies depending on the golfer's ability to visualize or conceptualize the shape of the shot. They are often more geometrical in their thinking. That is, they think in terms of angles, or stance or shoulders or position of their feet. They are more analytical than visual people. For example, to fade the ball to the target, they try to think as follows: if you line the feet and shoulders about 10 yards left of the target, have the face of the club a little open to the line, and swing a little left, then the ball will fade into the target. Their mental process is obviously more mechanically oriented than visually oriented. These golfers have a difficult time focusing on a target. They seem to lose perspective if they do. They know through long hours of practice and playing that to hit a fade, simply aim left and hold on with the left hand a little tighter. This prohibits a full release and shapes the shot in a left to right pattern.

There are many high school and college golf coaches who have their players occasionally play from the front tees, to get them used to shooting low scores. This approach can be a good object lesson for the players. It allows them to get used to the positive feeling that if they get to one under par, they then can think about two under par. And if they get to two under, think three under and so on. This method can provide many of the players with a one-time breakthrough – that they will no longer simply protect their score. Along with this approach, the players must be taught not to get ahead of themselves, and to stay in the present. Stay focused on the moment. This approach can provide the players with a stronger mental discipline and better state of mind. They won't worry about shooting low scores. They may start to think about birdieing every hole. Think 54! Pia Nielsen, the well-known Swedish golf instructor would talk to her students about shooting 18 under par. The byword for the students was 54. When some of her students would get to six under, they would be thinking seven under. They wouldn't get nervous about shooting a low number. The ultimate goal was 54. They were thinking positive thoughts like, play aggressively to a conservative target, and stay on the offense. They were not thinking to protect their score. The more low scores you shoot, the easier it is (mentally) the next time you are in a low scoring situation. Always think that you can go lower.

This reminds me of a story that happened about 35 years ago. There were sixteen of us who used to have an annual tournament called "The Flog." Flog is golf spelled backwards. We were all single digit or scratch players. Normally, we had our event at Pebble Beach and we stayed at the Lodge. The event was 72 holes and was very competitive. After three rounds, I was tied for the lead despite the fact that I had not been putting up to my standards. As a matter of fact, I was very tentative and nervous. Perhaps, you could call it a borderline case of the Yipps. Anyway, the fourth round gave me my best start ever on a golf course. After hitting a 7-iron approach to 20 feet above the pin on the first hole, I left my first putt eight feet short and downhill. I began to think that this was going to be another one of those trying days. I mustered up all of the courage that I had and willed the ball into the hole for a par. On the second hole, a par five, my approach was just off of the left edge of the green, and I chipped it in for an eagle. I got a routine par at number three. And, then I birdied numbers four, five and six.

So there I was standing on the famous, short 100-yard seventh hole at Pebble Beach at five under par. I was really nervous standing on that tee. I changed clubs two or three times. I finally selected a 9-iron and promptly dribbled it into the front bunker. Bogey. I also hit my second shot out of bounds at the fourteenth hole and had to hit a four-wood for my third shot at the eighteenth hole. Despite the bad shots, I managed to win the "Flog" by one shot. I mention this story because even though I didn't know it then, but I realize now that my great round was essentially over on the seventh tee because I was trying to protect my score. I did not have the experience at that time to keep trying to get my score lower. I should have been thinking, I am five under, now let's get to six under. Never protect. It is like the prevent defense in football. It will make you lose more often than not.

The following are a few examples of course management. We will use a hypothetical character, named Billy Birdie. Billy is in contention for winning a golf event. He is coming down the stretch two shots back of the lead with three holes to play. Look at the illustrations at the end of this section. The par 3, 16th hole is a dangerous one. Billy's normal shot is a controlled fade. He can fade the ball nine times out of ten. He is not as successful when he tries to draw the ball (his success rate is roughly 60% of the time.) Even though it is a "sucker" pin placement, he wants to win the event and decides to be aggressive. He feels that he can control the aggressiveness. He decides to play a three-quarter 8-iron and hold it against the wind. A crisp shot should carry just past the pin into the rise of the green and spin back towards the pin. He is totally focused on the shot and fully committed to it. The execution comes off as planned and the ball comes to rest four feet below the pin. He gets a birdie. (Billy has played to his strength.)

The 17th hole is made to order for Billy. There is a 10-15 mile-an-hour slice crosswind. The birdie on the 16th gave Billy a confidence rush. He made up his mind to hit his "bread and butter" shot. He had no doubt and hit a hard fade aimed at the left bunker. The drive ended up in the center of the fairway, 156 yards from the pin. The pin placement was easily accessible for Billy's approach shot. He hit a little 7-iron that finished pin high, 16 feet right of the pin. The putt was a little down grain and slightly downhill. After studying it, he decided to play it about three balls outside the right edge. The putt was perfect for another birdie. Now there is only one more hole to play. (Billy knew he had to get the ball into the fairway, and, when he did, the 7-iron fade was the ideal shot for the situation. Again, he played to his strength.)

The 18th hole is a reachable par five, but its design created a little anxiety for Billy since his normal shot pattern was a fade. Billy took a little extra time focusing on the shot. His best percentage shot was to go with the fade, knowing full well that he would have to start it out over the edge of the water, a very dangerous play. But, then again, he hit a fade nine times out of ten. His other option, to draw the shot off of the deep bunker that guarded the right side of the dogleg, was not a good play for him. If he hit the ball into this bunker, he would have to wedge it back to the fairway, thereby reducing his chances for birdie. He knew that he needed to make a birdie to have a chance to win the event. He was only one stroke behind the leader when he stepped onto the 18th tee. Billy hit it hard and the shot ended up in the fairway 234 yards from the front of the green. The pin was another 12 paces away. Now, Billy knew that he would have to hit a solid 3-wood to have an eagle opportunity. His 3-wood second shot was a good one that just made the front edge of the green. Billy was faced with a 40 foot, side-hill curling putt. He did two-putt for a birdie. However, the leader also birdied the hole and Billy placed second. (Billy knew the risks and rewards. He played to his strengths. He maintained his focus. He applied the principles of **F-A-C-E**.)

Nothing compares to being in the zone. The more you can get there, the better it is for your game. You will really appreciate what the game is all about, and enjoy it so much more. In this chapter, you were provided with some insight on how to get there. Work on these principles and concepts and watch your game improve.

16th Hole

Par 3.

155 yards to the middle of the green, which has pin located 143 yards from the tee and is on the lower level of the green. (This is known as the "sucker" pin placement.

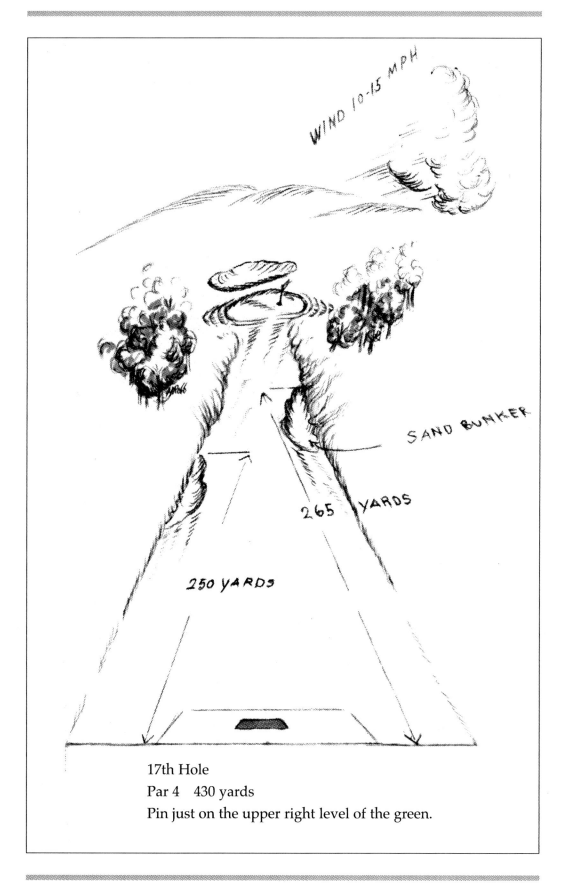

WIND 10-15 MPH

SAND BUNKER

265 YARDS

250 YARDS

17th Hole

Par 4   430 yards

Pin just on the upper right level of the green.

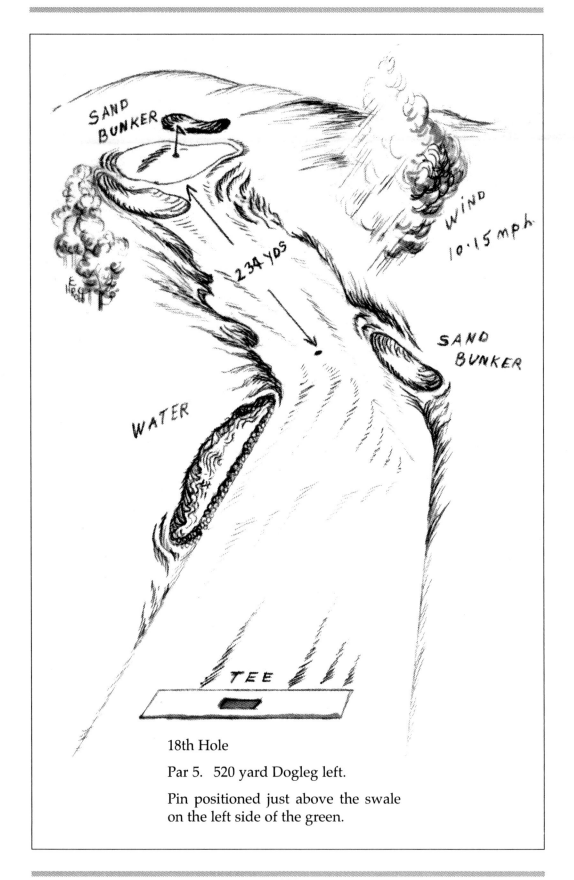

SAND BUNKER

WIND 10·15 mph

234 YDS

WATER

SAND BUNKER

TEE

18th Hole

Par 5. 520 yard Dogleg left.

Pin positioned just above the swale
on the left side of the green.

CHAPTER 5
PRACTICE

The quality of your practice sessions is much more important than the quantity. It isn't the number of balls that you hit, it is how disciplined you are when hitting them. Hitting ball after ball can relieve frustration and tension, and occasionally you may need to do that, but the majority of your practice time should be quality oriented. A practice session should begin with some warm-up stretching exercises and end with five to seven minutes of playing shots as if you were on the golf course. Go through your entire process, including the pre-shot routine and applying the principles of **F-A-C-E**. In between the beginning and the end, you should start with your short irons and work up to the driver. Then you can practice chipping and putting afterwards.

Over the years, I have had the good fortune to practice and play with a number of professional tour players. I watched and learned from their practice habits. They are very disciplined and all business when they practice. They work on the specific parts of their game that need improvement. Many of them have specific drills that help counter-balance any flaws or tendencies in their swing. For example, they may have a tendency to get their hips too far out in front when they try to hit the ball too far. Or they may tilt their shoulders too much on the backswing. They are continually monitoring these tendencies. The trajectory of the ball or the pattern of their divot can give them the necessary feedback to let them know what took place during the swing. It may be something in their swing that just doesn't feel right. They might then check out their stance, posture and balance. They may simply be trying out different clubs. No matter how long a professional spends on the practice tee, it is quality time.

The average golfer is about a 15 handicap. He often doesn't have the time or the desire to spend a lot of time on the practice tee. Every golfer should answer the following questions. How much are you willing to practice? How much do you want to improve? If you were investing your money, wouldn't you have a short- and long- term plan? Why shouldn't you do the same for your golf game? When you go to your teaching professional or golf instructor, do you want the Band-Aid approach (short term), or do you want to learn a method to really improve your game long term? Look for an instructor who can explain remedies that apply to your particular swing. Observing professionals with similar body swings can be helpful. If you are a lower body swinger, you should be receiving information that is aimed more toward the lower body sequencing. For example, watch the swings of Nicklaus and Trevino. If you are an upper body player, look at Watson, Stadler, and Sutton. If you are a hands high swinger study Larry Mize; or, if your swing is short and compact and you are a body rotator, watch Tiger Woods or Paul Azinger. Have an instructor isolate your faults, explain why you have them, and tell you what to do to correct them.

Your instructor should provide you with drills that can help you overcome your tendencies in a non-manipulative fashion. For example, with a club held in front of you about hip high, swing it back and forth to a full finish. Each time you swing it back and forth, lower the swing toward the ground. Never let the club head touch the ground. Then, step up to the ball keeping your club head off of the ground and start your backswing in the same way that you were swinging the club in the drill. Just let the ball get in the way. Trust it. This is a simple drill that can, with repetition, become very useful. It can help relieve tension and ball consciousness and give you an easier way to trigger your swing. It should smooth your swing and make it very rhythmic. It can also help teach you how to swing the club and not manipulate it. Take it to the course and implement it. It will help you to swing within yourself on the course. Keep it simple. (See Baseball Swing Drill illustrations.)

To gain the rewards of golf, you must play smart golf. Not just with the mental aspects of the game, but the physical as well. On the range, determine how far you fly the ball in the air with each of your clubs. When on the course, it is important to know the distances to the front and back of the greens, distances to carry over bunkers, lakes, streams and so on. You should also know the contours of the greens, their shelves, severe slopes, etc. On an approach shot, know where on the green your ball should be in order to have the best putt for a birdie or par. Pick targets off of the golf course, such as church spires, mountain peaks, or clouds to help align your shots.

Whether or not you have had a long layoff from the game, it is important that you begin your practice sessions with the proper alignment, posture and stance. After your stretching warm-up, choose a target and lay two clubs down on the ground parallel to one another, like the railroad tracks. Make this a habit. Professional golfers do it, so why not you? The majority of amateur golfers address the ball with improper alignment. That is why they have a hard time getting the ball started on the proper line. This alignment technique is simple to do, and vital to improving your game.

Baseball Swing Drill (A)

Hold the club out in front of you as shown. Make a full swing on the same plane.

Baseball Swing Drill (A)

Baseball Swing Drill (A)

Baseball Swing Drill (A)

Baseball Swing Drill (B)

Lower the club from the hip high position and repeat the swing on the new plane.

Baseball Swing Drill (B)

Baseball Swing Drill (B)

Baseball Swing Drill (B)

We have discussed the importance of correct posture, stance and center of gravity, which controls your balance during the swing. Because of its importance, we are going to include the center of gravity/balance drill again by way of illustration. Remember that if your balance is not correct during the swing, mis-hits will occur, but the reason why will not be easy to determine. How often have you felt that you made a good swing, yet you hit the shot on the neck of the club? It is usually the result of poor balance at the top of the swing. For example, at the top of the backswing, if your weight is more toward the toes of your feet, your upper body is out over your lower body. The result is a weak, neck shot. You should always feel planted into the ground when you take your stance. Feel as if you were going to shoot a free throw in basketball. If you are not comfortable over the ball, have someone check out your posture. Without the correct stance, posture and balance, you can't improve. It is that simple.

Let's review what to do with respect to your stance, set up and alignment.

- Position the ball opposite the left instep.

- Set the shoulders, hips and feet parallel to the target line.

- Set the right foot perpendicular (square) to the line.

- Flare out your left foot about 30 degrees from the target line. This will help you to get better torsion or coiling between the hips and shoulders on the backswing and allow for a freer clearing of the hips on the through-swing.

- Distribute your weight equally on the inside of both feet.

- Flex both knees inward and maintain the flex in the knees throughout the swing.

- Bend slightly from the waist, keeping the back relatively straight. Do not crouch or bend over too much, as it will inhibit a full turn back and upset your center of gravity. It also offsets your balance and prohibits you from getting your body out of the way on the through-swing.

- Let the arms hang naturally from the shoulder sockets. Do not reach for the ball, as that can create tension in the arms, wrists, and hands.

- Align the left arm and club to form a straight line to the ball.

- Keep the wrists and hands relaxed. Do not arch the wrists.

Another good habit to develop is the rehearsal swing. Make it a simulation of the actual swing you intend to use. That will provide you with a sense of purpose for learning how to execute shots. It also can provide you with feedback as to your set up, posture, and balance prior to the shot. For example, let's say that you were planning to draw the ball into the green with a 6-iron. In your rehearsal swing, you would aim slightly right of the target, close your stance, and make a one-piece takeaway that would go back slightly inside your line. Visualize the shape of the shot. Commit to it. Then step up to the ball, and make a smooth, rhythmic swing. Once you get into the habit of simulating your shot with a rehearsal swing, you will become more and more comfortable with the process. It should become an integral part of your pre-shot routine. The rehearsal forces you to think positively and get your thought processes in order. And, since the thought process is taking place prior to the swing, the actual swing's execution should be instinctive. The rehearsal can also speed up your play and improve your shotmaking skills. I have seen this improvement time after time.

Railroad Tracks — Driver

Set two clubs down on the ground parallel to one another as shown. This helps you to align yourself properly. When you change targets, reset the alignment of the clubs.

Railroad Tracks — 5-Iron

Set Up, Alignment and Ball Positioning

Place three clubs on the ground, as shown, to get your proper alignment and ball positioning when you hit balls on the practice tee.

Center of Gravity/Balance Check

At the top of the backswing, the golfer had too much weight toward his toes as demonstrated by him losing balance from a gentle push from behind at the beltline.

Center of Gravity/Balance Check

Again at the top, by tugging backward and downward slightly on the golfer's beltline, the golfer was stabilized.

Center of Gravity/Balance Check

A gentle push at the beltline does not throw the golfer off balance.

There are several other advantages to the simulation procedure. It helps you "swing within yourself," which increases the probability of successful execution of the shot. It can also help you make a more graceful swing. You are swinging, not hitting. It helps to eliminate ball consciousness, fear, anxiety, and tension. Most of all, it builds confidence, because your actual swing, if it mirrors your simulated swing, will be smooth and include a good releasing action, which is the essential ingredient for solid contact and crisp shots.

Golf is a game of angles. To produce a draw or fade, the direction of the swing and club face alignment through the impact area are varied slightly from the square position. Remember that with the driver, a two-degree misalignment from the square position represents about a 15 to 20 yard deviation from the middle of the fairway, given a 100 miles-per-hour swing speed. One simple instructional approach to help golfers hit draws or fades, is the "catcher's mitt" method. Imagine that you are a batter at the plate hitting a baseball thrown by a pitcher. Further imagine that the catcher is giving the pitcher a spot or target where he wants the pitcher to throw the ball. The catcher uses his mitt for the target, i.e., low and outside of home plate, right down the middle of the plate, or low and inside the plate.

Now, let's translate this concept to a golfer at address. First, we are going to assume that the golfer has the correct address, set up, posture and alignment. And, that he is not a beginner.

If the golfer wants to hit the ball straight down the middle of the fairway, he tries to put the club head directly into the middle (or pocket) of the catcher's mitt in a one-piece low and straight movement of the club head. A full turn back behind the ball to the top of the backswing, and a pulling and firing move through the ball, most likely, should promote solid contact and a relatively straight golf shot.

For a draw shot, set the left foot slightly closed to the line. Your alignment should be slightly to the right of your target. Make a one-piece takeaway and have the club head hit the inside edge of the catcher's mitt. Go ahead and make your normal swing. Trust it. As a result of the altered set up and hitting the catcher's mitt on the inside of the intended line, the ball should start to the right and draw toward the target due to the club face being in a slightly closed position at impact.

For a fade shot, set the left foot slightly open to the line. Your alignment should be slightly to the left of your target. This alignment allows for the left to right flight that is desired to hit the fade. Make a one-piece takeaway and hit the outside edge of the catcher's mitt with the club head. Make your normal swing and trust it. The club face should impact the ball in a slightly open position causing the ball to have the proper left to right flight.

This is a very simple way to learn how to work the ball left or right, high or low. This "catcher's mitt" drill really works.

Another exercise to implement into your practice sessions is the "eyes shut monitoring system" (ESMS). When you include this exercise into your practices, you will notice an improvement in the quality of your practice time. Once you understand the basic fundamentals of the swing and use the ESMS, the feedback received will provide you with increased knowledge of your swing. You will be able to detect your faults or fault patterns easier and begin to cure them more quickly. Remember that it is cause and effect. For example, let's say that you are reaching for the ball and gripping the club to tight. This can cause your hands, arms and shoulders to have too much tension. Normally, this will result in a fast, jerky takeaway instead of the one-piece movement that is desired for a free flowing swing. Reaching for the ball can also cause other problems, such as blocked shots, or weak slices. The reason for this is that you are stooped over the ball too much, which destroys your balance during the swing, inhibits a full turn on the backswing, and makes it difficult to get your body out of the way in the through-swing. The ESMS can help you with the early detection of such problem areas. Monitor your comfort level at address. Are you relieved of tension? Are you getting a full turn on the backswing? Is your sternum over the right knee at the top, and over your left knee at the finish?

Catcher's Mitt Drill — Straight Shot

Using a one-piece takeaway, push the club head into the center of the catcher's mitt to hit a straight line.

Catcher's Mitt Drill — Fade

Using a one-piece takeaway, push the club head to the outside edge of the catcher's mitt for a fade shot.

Catcher's Mitt Drill — Draw

Using a one-piece takeaway, push the club head to the inside edge of the catcher's mitt for a draw shot.

Use the ESMS to monitor the baseball drill mentioned earlier. Observe the freedom in the swing. Listen to the "swoosh" of the club head while you are swinging freely. Monitor your body parts during your practice swings. During one swing, monitor your foot action or balance throughout the swing. Feel the weight transfer from one foot to another. Is it transferring to the inside of the right foot while you are going back? Is it re-transferring to the inside of the left foot while in the impact area? Is the left leg maintaining its flex during impact or is it rigid? (If the left leg stiffens during impact, this can inhibit your lower body rotation through the ball and result in a blocked shot.)

During another swing, monitor your hip turn. On other swings, monitor the shoulder turn, your wrist action, extension, width, the pulling action of the left arm, the firing of the right side, and so on. Do this with your eyes closed. It provides positive feedback and wonderful insight. Still, you must first understand the basic fundamentals of the sequencing of the golf swing.

WARM-UP EXERCISES

Prior to hitting balls at the range, you should do a few simple loosening-up exercises. At the very least, do the following exercises. First, hold a driver or fairway wood at each end and place it behind your neck. Then slowly make a full turn back and hold it for one or two seconds. Then, make a forward turn to a full finish and hold for one or two seconds. Repeat this four or five times. Remember to do it slowly. A second exercise requires that you take two or three short irons and swing them slowly back and forth as if you were swinging a heavy golf club. Make sure that you are swinging above the ground and swinging slowly. Allow your hands and wrists to be relaxed while you are swinging. Feel the weight of the heads of the clubs. This is more than just a warm-up drill. It can help you with your rhythm and tempo. In the third warm-up, hold two or three short irons in your right hand at your side just below the grips and vertical to the ground. Then, swing your arm in a circle forward and backward two or three times; then reverse the circle and go backward to forward. Then, change hands and repeat the drill. This drill loosens the shoulder sockets. In the fourth warm-up you use a driver, held at the ends, and bend over from the waist until you almost touch the ground. Keep you knees relatively straight. Then extend the driver over your head and back behind you and hold for one or two seconds. Then, return to your original position. Repeat this drill three times. These simple drills only take a few minutes, but they will help you to limber up the proper muscles before you begin hitting golf balls. Be sure to do them before you play, especially if you don't have a chance to get to the practice range. The older you get, the more important it is to do proper warm-up exercises.

There is another set of stretching exercises that you can do with three-foot surgical tubing. It can be purchased from a medical supply store, and you can take it with you on business trips or keep it in your golf bag. First, grasp the tubing near the ends and stretch it out holding it behind your neck and just touching your shoulders. With your feet close together, make a full turn back and through. Do this eight to 10 times. The second exercise begins with you holding the tubing behind you, and extending your right arm skyward so that your shoulder almost touches the right ear. At the same time, let your left arm extend downward toward your left side. Then reverse the arm positions. Do this 10 times. For the third exercise, grasp the tubing close to its ends and extend your arms directly in front of you. Then, while keeping the arms straight, extend them over your head and back behind you. Do this slowly. Be careful not to strain yourself when you first begin. Only extend back as far as is comfortable. Then re-extend your arms in front of you. Do this 10 times.

Always begin your practice sessions with short irons. Pick a target, don't just hit for the sake of hitting. As a general rule, hit three or four shots at the same target, then change targets. Do this with all of the clubs that you normally use, as you work through the bag. The last seven to 10 minutes of your practice should be reserved for shotmaking. Use the principles of **F-A-C-E.** Focus on the target and visualize the shape of the shot that you want to hit. Make a full commitment to the shot and then Execute with a full, free swing. Get into the habit of the "catcher's mitt" method to work the ball.

Stretching Drills

With a driver or fairway wood, place the club behind your back and inside your elbows. Then turn back and point the end of the club's handle toward the ball as shown.

Stretching Drills

Holding the club as shown, turn through to a full finish. Make sure your weight is almost entirely on the left foot.

Stretching Drills

With a driver or fairway wood, bend from the waist while holding the club as shown. Hold this position for 2-3 seconds. Repeat this drill three times.

Stretching

Hold two clubs behind your shoulders as shown. Then make a full stretch back. And a full stretch through. Hold each position for two seconds. Do this three times. (Depending upon your flexibility, you may have to use fairway woods to do this stretching exercise.)

Stretching

Stretching

Warm Up Drill

Take two or three short irons and loosen up by swinging back and through as shown. Do not swing hard but swing to a finish. Allow your wrists to cock and uncock freely.

Warm Up Drill

Warm Up Drill

Warm Up Drill

Warm Up Drill

Warm Up Drill

Hold two short irons at the base of the grip and loosen the shoulder sockets as shown. Swing your arm forward and backward in a circular motion.

Warm Up Drill

Warm Up Drill

CHAPTER 6
FOR WOMEN GOLFERS –
HIT IT LONGER WITH LESS EFFORT

Women golfers are very active participants in golf today. Because of their physical nature, women golfers, on the average, do not hit the ball a long way. Even though the average weekend male golfer may hit the ball farther than most women, when they get to within 100 yards of the green, many factors suggest that they are at a disadvantage to women. Most women have a marvelous sense of touch on shots within short distances from the green, while many male golfers seem to have hands made of stone. This sense of touch can overpower the distance factor. In this chapter, we provide you with explanatory illustrations that give you a perspective on how to gain more distance. Whether you are a beginner or a more serious player, more distance is within your grasp.

Recognizing that the scores of most women golfers range between 90 and 115, this chapter will provide you with the fundamentals for a graceful swing so that you can lower your scores. The illustrations in this section will provide you with the foundation for a solid, basic swing. It will be up to you to spend the time necessary to improve your game.

In Chapter 3, I mentioned Harry Pressler's "over and under" swing method for women golfers, including LPGA professionals. This method is not only simple, but also a very effective learning tool. It forces a player to swing the club in the proper path. The illustrations clearly demonstrate this method. We use a simple training aid (an elastic wrap) in some of the illustrations to emphasize maintaining a proper triangle.

Remember that all of the fundamentals in the preceding chapters apply to all golfers. You must still have a good grip, stance, posture, alignment and pre-shot routine to make a solid swing at the ball. In addition, you must know and understand the sequence of the swing, know how to groove it and be able to work out any swing flaws that you may have. We are not going to repeat the basic fundamentals in this chapter. However, some modifications are suggested for women only, so that they can get a little more power into the ball. For example, with respect to the grip, it is suggested that women golfers experiment with a stronger grip. Let the "V's" point to about halfway between the chin and the tip of your right shoulder. With respect to the left hand, grip the club more in the fingers to get more snap at impact, while still keeping it firm in the last three fingers because these three fingers keep the club under control at the top of the backswing. You will find a number of other suggestions in the text of the illustrations.

Always try to play intelligent golf. Know the yardage to carry obstacles. Pick smart targets. Play to your strengths. Know the contour, slope and speed of the greens. Know if there are subtle breaks in the greens and the best spot on the green to give yourself a better chance to make a putt. Know the trouble around the greens. Keep a journal or record of your play. It will help you to evaluate your progress and assist you in what to work on during your practice sessions.

Make sure you know your distances for each club. For your convenience, a Table of Distances is provided at the end of the book. Always take enough club to get to your target. For example, let's say that you fly your 7-iron 80 yards and your 6-iron 90 yards. Assume that you are 85 yards to the front of the green and the pin is on the green another five yards. But, the green is severely sloped from back to front and it is fast. The objective in this situation would be to keep the ball below the hole. Therefore, the prudent shot would be to hit the 7-iron and if you got a bounce in front of the green, the shot would put you on the front of the green underneath the hole. This would be the ideal play to make birdie or par. If you elected to hit your 6-iron and hit it solidly, you would fly the ball about pin-high and if you got a bounce, you would end up above the hole and have a very difficult two-putt. Most likely, it would result in a three-putt green. That is exactly what you don't need. So when you hear the expression, always take enough club, it means to take enough club to make the intelligent shot. Even if your ball ended up short of the green in this situation, your chance of making par is better than if your ball is above the cup.

Do not guess about how far you fly the ball. Know your distances for a calm, clear day. Remember that your distances will vary depending on course conditions, i.e., wet or dry, soft or firm fairways, wind, your physical condition and so on. The more you play, the easier it becomes to factor other conditions into your yardage measurements.

In the following illustrations, please observe how the golfer adheres to the fundamental principles detailed in other chapters of this book. Note how well she sets up to the ball and works back behind it. She gets a wonderful coiling of the upper torso. Notice how it is balanced over the lower body, and how steady her head is throughout the swing.

Planted at address. She is comfortable over the ball and "sitting to it." The upper body is bent slightly from the waist, and her back is relatively straight. The spinal column is tilted slightly to her right. This is her axis of rotation. Her knees are flexed and her right knee is pointed slightly inward. Her feet are well planted into the ground. The weight is evenly distributed on the inside of both feet. The triangle formed by the hands, arms and shoulders is relaxed and she has the proper tilt. This is a powerful address position. She is not rigid or stiff.

Stay planted throughout the swing. In the illustrations with the elastic wrap training aid, notice that the graceful one-piece takeaway is low and slow. The one-piece takeaway sets the swing in motion. It is probably the most important thing to get right in starting the swing. The elastic wrap training aid promotes this movement. (All golfers should have one of these wraps. They are easy to make. Buy a piece of elastic band about two to four inches wide and about 24-inches long and sew the ends together to fit your physical build. The one used in the illustrations is about 10 1/2 inches in diameter.) The extension of the arms begins to pull the hips into their turn on the backswing. The left knee breaks inward and points behind the ball as the left foot rolls on its instep. She is turning nicely around her slightly tilted axis. Notice the right side as it loads (accepts) the weight transfer. There is no sway off of the ball. Observe how she is covering the ball and still sitting to it. Her head is rock steady. The hands remain passive.

Work back behind the ball. Observe the golfer at the top of the backswing. Notice that her sternum is over the right knee. Her back is facing the target. Her right leg, knee, foot and hip joint are fully loaded on the inside of each part, meaning that the weight has been transferred from her left side and loaded to her right side. It never gets to the outside of her right side. If it did, she would lose power. There is no sway. The momentum of the backswing has set the club at the top. The upper torso is coiled over the lower body. The left shoulder is tilted down and her shoulder is under the chin. She has made a full turn or pivot around her tilted axis, her spinal column. Her head is still quiet and steady. She is coiled for power.

The Drive
Frame 1

Comfort at address.

The Drive
Frame 2

One-piece takeaway.

The Drive
Frame 3

A full turn, the right side is fully "loaded". Notice that the right leg is not locked. It still has flex to it.

The Drive
Frame 4

The "bump" and "drop" has occurred.

The Drive
Frame 5

The "pulling" and "firing" are taking place. The left hip has cleared and the left leg is braced for the contact of the club with the ball at impact.

The Drive
Frame 6

Note the full extension of the arms down the line. The right side has fired completely and poured on the power.

The Drive
Frame 7

The full, well-balanced finish is a result of a solid, properly sequenced swing. Note the steady head throughout the swing.

Staying behind the ball until after impact. The through-swing begins with a coordinated lower body movement. Some golfers feel that their hips begin turning to the left and have a slight lateral move of about four to six inches. This move is referred to as "bump" and "drop." In other words, there is a slight "bump" of the hips to the left, and this bump "drops" the club into the slot to start down. Other golfers feel that the left foot is returned to its original position at address. Still others believe that they re-roll their weight back onto the inside of their left foot. In any case, the unified or coordinated lower body movement is responsible for the beginning of the through-swing. It is this move that begins the re-transfer of weight back to the left side. The shoulders, arms and hands, in that order, then release their stored-up energy. At impact, the left arm essentially returns to its position at address and is fully extended while the right arm is still slightly bent. Through the impact zone, the golfer should feel that the club head is going right at the target.

Let the momentum of the swing bring you to a full finish. Note that the left arm and hand are still in control of the club through impact and beyond. This control allows you to power the ball with the right hand at impact. And, there is no fear of hitting wild hooks. Both arms straighten out about hip high on the follow-through. The momentum of the swing brings her to a full, well-balanced finish.

Generally speaking, if you swing the club smoothly and with good rhythm, you will make solid contact with the ball. This assumes, of course, good set up, posture, aim and alignment. Being relaxed in the hands, wrists, arms and shoulders that form the triangle, is the key to swinging with rhythm and power. Tension can cause a fast, jerky swing resulting in a weak shot, poor release action of the club, and lunging at the ball. Most importantly, it makes you "press" for more distance, which destroys rhythm and timing. Use your suppleness to help you learn to swing the woods and irons. Always try to swing within yourself with good rhythm. You should always swing at the ball, not lunge at it.

The golf swing is not just brute power. The swing is the thing. Swing within yourself but get a good windup on the backswing to allow an accelerated move through the ball. Most good golfers "throttle back" on iron shots. They swing within themselves at about 80% to 85% of their full power. By doing this, they get solid contact, direction and control.

Wendy Stuart, an assistant club professional, modeled for the illustrations shown. I thank her for her time and patience. Study these photographs carefully. Go to the practice tee and implement the techniques shown. The illustrations and accompanying text demonstrate:

- Set up, posture and balance.
- The waggle
- The extension necessary for a good takeaway.
- The left arm control and "pulling" action.

- The feet-close-together drill.

- The "over and under" drill using a training aid. It shows the one-piece takeaway and the "pulling" and "firing" action using the aid.

- The full swing for the driver.

- A down-the-line view of her "crushing the drive."

- The pre-shot routine procedure.

- A frontal view of "loading" and "firing."

- A view from behind the golfer's back of "loading" and "firing."

Good luck in lowering your scores and hitting it long and straight with less effort. Try to make the moves that Wendy makes in these illustrations or use them to identify differences between your swing and hers.

Set Up and Posture — Three Views

- Comfortable and well-balanced

- The triangle formed by the hands, arms and shoulders is relaxed.

- The golfer has the proper tilt.

- The weight is evenly distributed on the inside of both feet.

- The knees are flexed and legs are springy.

- The arms are hanging freely and the hands are underneath the shoulders.

- The distance between the club handle and the legs is about six inches.

- The back is straight and she is bent slightly from the waist.

This setup promotes good balance throughout the swing. Note: The golfer has a strong grip where the "V's" point about halfway between the chin and the tip of her right shoulder. A strong grip is suggested for most women golfers.

The Waggle

- The golfer is rehearsing the beginning of her swing through the use of the waggle.

- The waggle is a tension reliever.

- It promotes a one-piece take-away which sets the swing into the proper sequence.

Extension

The golfer has started her backswing with a comfortable extension of the left arm. There is ample stretching without any sign of tension. The relaxed triangle formed at address allows this comfortable extension.

"Pulling" of the Left Arm
Frame 1

At the top of the backswing is the critical point. The hands at the top should never be loosened. The last three fingers of the left hand secure the club at the top. The right hand should just be along for the ride. The average woman golfer seems to re-grip or cast the club from the top with her hands.

"Pulling" of the Left Arm
Frame 2

Starting down, the hands have remained in their same relative position as they were at the top. The first move from the top is a reversal of the hips or a turning of them counterclockwise. The slight movement, known as the "bump" and "drop" move, causes the arms and hands to drop the club into the slot or the hitting area. The left arm is beginning its pulling action; it pulls down.

Frame 3

Frame 4

Frame 5

Frame 6

Frame 7

Frame 8

Feet Close Together Drill

This is a very good drill for getting the feeling for the arm swing. By practicing this drill the golfer can make the releasing action automatic while overcoming any fear or anxiety she may have. It also helps eliminate the tension that some golfers have from being overly ball conscience.

Take a pitching wedge or short iron for this drill.

- Take your normal grip.

- Set up with your feet close together.

- Take a three-quarter swing back and three-quarter through-swing. Maintain your balance.

- Repeat this back and through motion with your eyes closed. Maintain your balance.

- Monitor the action of the body as it rotates back (winds-up) and through (unwinds). Continue swinging this way and monitor the arms, wrists and hands. Also, monitor your feet, knees and leg action as your swing back and forth.

- After you do this for a few minutes, you should being to feel how the body rotation (especially the hips) is central to the swinging action of the arms and hands and the full releasing action.

- Once you get this feeling, hit balls using this three-quarter swinging action. Keep your feet close together and stay in balance.

- Finally, using the same action, begin taking full swings with you normal stance.

**Over and Under Drill
Frame 1**

Using an elastic wrap that is two inches to four inches in width and 10 1/2 inches in diameter, hit three-quarter and full shots as shown. Use short irons at first. Place the wrap just above the elbows.

Note how well the triangle is formed.

**Over and Under Drill
Frame 2**

An excellent one-piece takeaway starts the swing into motion.

**Over and Under Drill
Frame 3**

The left arm is swinging over her breasts to the top. She has great width at the top.

Over and Under Drill
Frames 4,5,6

See how the right arm is coming down under the breasts. Note how well the left arm is pulling and the right elbow hugs the body down and through impact.

Over and Under Drill
Frame 7

Good arm extension down the line. These illustrations demonstrate the "pulling" and "firing" needed for power and direction.

Over and Under Drill — A down the line view using the training aid.

Impact Positions — Without the Training Aid

Compare the impact positions of the golfer with and without the training aid. They compare favorably.

Impact Positions

Impact Positions

Crushing the Drive — A Down the Line View
Frame 1

Set up to deliver a strong blow to the ball.

Crushing the Drive — A Down the Line View
Frame 2

Good relaxed extension with a one-piece takeaway.

Crushing the Drive — A Down the Line View
Frame 3

Notice how well the shaft of her club is loaded at the top. This is ideal at the top. The right leg is loaded. A full shoulder turn. Left wrist flat. The club is square.

Crushing the Drive — A Down the Line View
Frame 4

Through impact — a full release of the body and the club.

Crushing the Drive — A Down the Line View
Frame 5

Balanced finish. The natural completion of a solid swing.

Pre-Shot Routine

- Stand six to eight feet directly behind the ball in line with your chosen target.

- Visualize the type and shape of the shot you want to play.

- Walk to your ball staying focused on your target. Note that some players pick a spot on the ground a few feet in front of the ball in line with their target. This is an easier way for them to get the club face aligned.

- Grip the club and then position your body to the line for the shape of the shot that you are going to play.

- Make sure that your grip and stance are comfortable.

- Then, take your waggle or forward press and trigger your swing. Do not second-guess yourself.

"Loading" and "Firing"—Frontal View Frame 1

The upper body is coiled over the lower body. There is no sway. The head is steady. The sternum is over the right knee indicating a full turn. A powerful windup results.

"Loading" and "Firing"—Frontal View Frame 2

At impact, notice the "firing" of the right side. The left arm has straightened and the right hand is pouring on the power. The "bracing" action is solid, yet flexed. She has the upward thrust that is so necessary for power.

"Loading" and "Firing"—View from Behind the Golfer's Back.

"Loading" and "Firing"—View from Behind

IN CONCLUSION

This book, *Golfing in the Zone: The Long Game,* was written to help all golfers become better players by lowering their scores. Many golfers don't believe that they can improve their performance dramatically. In reality, if they learn and trust the techniques presented in this book, amazing things will happen. To play good golf, golfers need to both lower their scores and enjoy the real pleasure and satisfaction that comes from playing the game.

Golfers tend to just go through the motions most of the time. They are content to send the ball on its way and hope for the best. This is not good enough. They need to spend more time evaluating and visualizing each shot so that they have a better chance of making a good shot. If golfers learn and understand the sequence of the swing, practice the easy-to-learn swing techniques shown in this book and implement a sound thought process to go along with proper mechanical fundamentals, they will quickly see their scores come down.

This book outlined the thought-mechanical processes needed to improve one's game. The sound mechanics and simple but effective pre-shot routine, will prove invaluable to the golfers who work at incorporating them into their game. Equally important is the information on how to practice more effectively, and how to troubleshoot your own swing. Mental processes necessary to prepare for and play any course should help golfers play within themselves, and stay out of trouble on the course. Some insight as to what professionals and other accomplished players think about and work on, along with some ideas on how women can improve their game are also important topics covered in this book.

What really sets this book apart, is that the golfer is not only provided these sound mechanical fundamentals but also the thought processes or mental procedures for successfully implementing them. The integration of this thought-mechanical procedure is what defines the process by which golfers can "get in the zone." This synergistic union is termed **F-A-C-E,** which stands for **F**ocus **A**nd **C**ommit to and **E**xecute the shot at hand.

I encourage you to play golf for the love of the game and have a positive belief in yourself. Golf should be played as a game. It should be fun. Golf is a unique sport in that it can be a means of relaxation, while at the same time it can be very demanding. Every golfer would like to have a full, fluid swing that is smooth and rhythmic. However, by spending the necessary time practicing the mechanical techniques and thought processes described in this book, you can still make a not-so-fluid swing an efficient swing. Efficient enough so that you can enjoy the game and score reasonably well. Keep the following Ten Commandments in mind as you play golf. They are rules and guidelines that can help all golfers enjoy their game more.

TEN COMMANDMENTS

1. Play golf for the love of the game.

2. Keep your emotions under control.

3. Focus on the moment.

4. Do not indulge in negative self-talk.

5. Think like a champion.

6. Accept the ups and downs of the game.

7. Commit to every shot.

8. Show respect for others.

9. Practice with a purpose.

10. Have a positive belief in yourself.

APPENDIX A

TABLE OF DISTANCES

CLUB	AVERAGE DISTANCE (YARDS)	YOUR DISTANCE (YARDS)
No. 1 - Driver	170	_____
No. 3 - Metal Wood	160	_____
No. 5 - Metal Wood	150	_____
No. 7 - Metal Wood	140	_____
No. 9 - Metal Wood	130	_____
No. 3 - Iron		_____
No. 4 - Iron		_____
No. 5 - Iron	120	_____
No. 6 - Iron	110	_____
No. 7 - Iron	100	_____
No. 8 - Iron	90	_____
No. 9 - Iron	80	_____
Pitching Wedge	70	_____
Sand Wedge	60	_____
Lob Wedge	50	_____

The Table of Distances shows average distances under normal conditions for the average female golfer. Jot down your distances so that your club selection can improve.

APPENDIX B

ARE THERE NEW METHODS?

Many modern day teaching methods are basically a re-hash of old teaching methods. Terminology has changed but that is about all. What follows are the paraphrased principles that Harry Vardon wrote about circa 1920. The author has made some annotations after each principle for comparative purposes.

- *The body should be easy and comfortable at address.* This principle has not changed one iota. Just watch the average golfer's practice swing. It is normally smooth and rhythmic, and free of tension. Then, as the golfer addresses the ball, he gets fidgety, bends over too much, has the feet to far apart, and in general, loses sight of the ease and comfort required of a good address position.

- *The stance should be open, with the rear foot square to the line of play and the leading foot angled toward the target.* Taking this statement literally, everyone should play with an open stance. But, on closer reflection, hasn't Mr. Vardon defined the stance that Ben Hogan popularized? That is, the right foot being square to the line, and the left foot being "flared out" a quarter of a turn (about 22 degrees).

- *The ball should be addressed opposite the left heel or, if not there, nearer to the left heel than the right – unless you wish to play a low shot.* Almost all tour-caliber players play the ball off of the instep of the left foot for normal shots.

- *I like my ankles to be free, which is why I play in shoes, not boots.* This is a sign of the times. Golf shoes, as we know them today, were non-existent. But, golfers should be able to wiggle their toes inside their shoes, which is another way of saying to have the ankles free, at address. This relieves tension.

- *When the club face is against the ball, the end of the shaft should reach to the flexed left knee.* Mr. Vardon is saying, "don't reach for the ball", which is still a modern day philosophy. Also, he did not grip the club handle at its end, he choked-up on the club.

- *The arms do not touch the body at address, but neither do they reach.* Another way of stating, measure to the ball and let the arms hang freely from the shoulder sockets. This is at slight variance to Jimmy Ballard's connection theory.

- *The weight should be divided equally between both feet.* Today, instructors still teach this concept but emphasize that the weight should be distributed on the insides of both feet.

- *It is necessary only to find the correct stance and the shot is certain to be a success.* What a great statement. Address, posture, and aiming and alignment, along with the ease and comfort of the stance are what it is all about for good shotmaking. Mr. Vardon also trusted his swing, which is obvious from this statement.

- *The head should be steady throughout the swing because if it moves, the body goes with it, disrupting the club's path.* A bedrock principle in golf – the steady or quiet head during the swing. All of the great players believe in this principle.

- *The eyes should be focused on the back of the ball or on the ground just to the right of the ball.* Keep your eyes on the ball. Swing the club and let the ball get in the way.

- *An upright swing offers the shortest and therefore the most efficient route from and to the ball.* Jack Nicklaus believed whole-heartedly in an upright swing. Mr. Vardon, who was a tall person, and his colleagues of that era, believed in the pendulum swing as being the most efficient. Ben Hogan popularized the swing plane theory, which is dependent upon the golfer's physical structure. Swinging in plane is efficient. And, if a golfer has the correct posture and center of gravity at address, he will be in the ideal swing plane.

- *Avoid straining for too wide a backswing, for if you do, you will likely sway your body.* This principle has not changed. The last thing a golfer wants to do is over-extend on the takeaway because it results in a loss of balance and power. When the clubshaft is horizontal to the ground on the backswing, the arms should be at their maximum comfortable extension. There should be no unnecessary tension.

- *The backswing is wound up by the swinging of the arms, the hips turning, and the left knee bending as the body pivots from the waist.* The modern theory is basically the same, i.e., the one-piece takeaway and pivoting around the right knee (or loading of the right side).

- *As the backswing proceeds, the right knee holds firm, but does not quite become stiff.* Keep the right knee flexed and pointed inward at address. And, maintain the flex in it at the top of the backswing. This prevents the sway and loads the right side.

- *Don't lift the left heel too much, but let it come comfortably up as you pivot onto the inside of the foot in response to your body pivot.* Roll on the inside of your left foot during the backswing. If you lift the heel of the left foot too high, you can reduce your coiling on the backswing, thus reducing power.

- *The grip relaxes a little as the backswing proceeds, especially the right hand.* This concept is different from the modern day theory. But, keep in mind, Mr. Vardon played with wooden-shafted clubs, not the steel or graphite ones of today. In his day, relaxing the grip on the backswing helped to get better loading of the wooden-shafted clubs and consequently, more snap at impact. Almost all of the players of that era "milked" the club at the top. Even the great Bobby Jones did it. With respect to the right hand, it is a good principle to have it soft or as relaxed as possible on the club from address to the top of the backswing. If the right hand is too tight on the club, it can cause tension along the right arm and right side of the body, which, in turn, can restrict the right side from "folding" easily on the backswing. It can also cause the golfer to "pick-up" or "lift" the club during the backswing, which reduces the full turn that is desired.

- *The right shoulder rises gradually as the body pivots. The body turns on its axis in the backswing and the downswing.* The same concept applies today. The golf swing is performed around a tilted axis of the spinal column.

- *There is no pause between the backswing and the downswing; they flow into each other.* Make a smooth transition from the top. The downswing actually begins with a lower body movement while the backswing is being completed. This move creates more torsion between the hips and the shoulders.

- *Don't jerk or snatch at the top or coming down or let the right wrist get on top of the club.* Let the hands be passive throughout the swing. Initiate the through-swing with a coordinated, lower body movement. Remember that the golfers of that era had to allow time for the "milking" of the club to take place.

- *The downswing is faster than the backswing, but there should be no conscious effort to make it so.* Take the club away low and slow in one piece. Feel as if you are accelerating through impact and beyond.

- *At its simplest, the swing is a matter of winding yourself up with your arms and unwinding yourself with your arms.* This principle hasn't changed. Modern players feel that they are coiling their upper body over their lower body on the backswing and re-coiling the lower body and the upper body (in that order) on the through-swing. The coiling is the result of swinging the arms to the top.

- *The grip automatically becomes firmer as the downswing proceeds.* Establish the correct grip pressure at address and make no conscious effort to change it throughout the swing.

- *Let the shoulder movement be steady and rhythmic, especially in the downswing.* The right shoulder lags the lower body throughout the swing, until the finish.

- *The club accelerates gradually to impact.* The maximum acceleration period during the swing takes place from hip to hip. That is, the golfer begins to release the club when it reaches his right hip on the downswing, and the acceleration continues until the club reaches hip high during the follow through. Science has determined that the maximum acceleration point of the club is slightly after impact with the ball. Feel as if you are accelerating all the way to a finish.

- *The wrists should be held firmly as the ball is hit. Do not bend the right wrist toward the target until after the ball has been struck.* Ben Hogan went a step further when he defined the supination of the left wrist bone.

- *At impact, the feet should be flat on the ground.* At impact, the left foot and leg are braced. The weight is on the inside of the left foot. Modern golfers have their right foot "firing" at the ball during impact. And, it normally does come off of the ground.

- *As the club goes through, the weight moves to the left, the left leg resists the blow, the right leg bends, the body fronts the line of flight, and the right foot raises almost vertically. At the finish, the arms are up, the hands are level with the head, the club beyond horizontal, and the body and shoulders face the target.* Impact and beyond. Quite a description for the bracing effect and a full, well-balanced finish.

- *I have always preferred an open stance because then I am not in the way of the club head as it swings through the ball. Also, an open stance encourages the upright swing that I favor.* Many tour players use an open stance. And, most of them are upright swingers, e.g., Nicklaus and Couples. Most, however use the square stance with the left foot flared out. Few tour players use a closed stance.

- *Don't scoop with the iron; thump down on it.* Modern theory accepts this principle. The exception, perhaps, may be with the long irons; most tour players sweep them.

- *The straight shot is difficult to repeat. Intentional pulls (hooks) and slices are golf's master shots.* Tour-caliber and accomplished players usually work the ball (fade or draw it) rather than try to hit a straight shot. If they normally fade the ball or draw it, they will play for their natural shot, as a general rule.

- *Good driving is the foundation of a good game. Learn to drive first with a Brassie, for it is easier than the Driver.* Today, instead of the Brassie, it would be a three-metal wood. Today's drivers are much easier to hit than in Mr. Vardon's day. But, driving is the foundation for good play. A good drive sets up the hole the way the architect intended it to be played.

- *I believe I use lighter clubs than many of my contemporaries. My Driver is forty-two inches long, and weighs twelve-and-three-quarter ounces; my Brassie is the same length but twelve ounces.* Lighter clubs are the foundation of modern day play for the average golfer, the accomplished player and the tour-caliber professional.

- *Never throw the club head or make a hit with it; swing it all the way.* The swing is the thing. Don't muscle the ball. Don't hit from the top.

- *There is no such thing as a pure wrist shot in golf, except for putting.* There are few wrist putters at the tour-caliber level of the game, except for a few Senior Tour players. Today, there can be pure wrist shots that can be played from very short greenside bunkers and some chips and lobs around the green. But, Mr. Vardon is correct about there being no pure wrist shot from the field.

- *The shorter the swing or the shot, the narrower the stance, the less the left foot and body action, and the more emphasis on the knees. The length of the backswing determines the distance of the less-than-full shot.* There is nothing especially new to add to these principles. Distance control is essential for short shots. Notice how many tour-caliber players are carrying three and four wedges in their bag. Using the "clock" method, i.e., 7:30 o'clock, 9:00 o'clock, and 10:30 o'clock with the left arm on the swing can control the distance on short shots.

- *The most successful way to play golf is the easiest way.* A perfect statement. Keep the swing mechanics simple. Keep the mind uncluttered.

- *To play well, you must feel tranquil and at peace. I have never been troubled by nerves in golf because I felt I had nothing to lose and all to gain.* Keep the mind uncluttered. Apply the principles of F-A-C-E to control the nerves. Focus And Commit to and Execute the shot at hand.

ABOUT THE AUTHOR

Ron DiZinno graduated with a degree from the School of Engineering at California State Polytechnic University. Currently, the author is a registered securities advisor licensed to practice in the state of California.

Ron resides in the town of La Quinta which is in the desert east of Los Angeles — a locale that provides an ideal climate for year-round golf. His widely acclaimed methods for both the short game and the long game are based on over 45 years of playing and teaching. He has worked with a number of club and tour professionals and other accomplished players.

Golfing in the Zone: The Long Game is also available on video. Ron's first book and video, *Golfing in the Zone: The Short Game*, are also available from Coaches Choice.